HOW TO ENJOY YOUR BIBLE

D1550204

HOW TO ENJOY YOUR BIBLE

JOHN BLANCHARD

 EVANGELICAL PRESS

EVANGELICAL PRESS
16—18 High Street, Welwyn, Hertfordshire,
AL6 9EQ, England.

First published 1978 by Henry Walter under the title
'Enjoy your Bible'.

First Evangelical Press edition 1984
Second impression 1987

ISBN 0 85234 182 2

Unless otherwise stated, all Bible quotations are from the
New International Version (Hodder & Stoughton, 1979)

Typeset in Great Britain by Inset, Hertford Heath.
Printed by Anchor Brendon Ltd., Tiptree, Colchester, England.

Contents

Introduction

This book is written out of two firmly held convictions.

The first is that the Bible is the Word of God. There was a time when the meaning of that statement would have been absolutely clear, incapable of being misunderstood, but in these days words are being made to mean almost anything, so let me explain myself. I am totally persuaded that every single word of the Bible's sixty-six books, in the form in which those books were originally written down by their various human authors, was 'God-breathed' (2 Timothy 3:16). This immediately speaks of the Bible's purity and unity. Its purity, that is to say its inerrancy and infallibility, is guaranteed by the fact that, God being God, his Word must necessarily be perfect in every way. But the Bible's divine authorship also guarantees its unity, each separate part contributing perfectly to all the others, because every one of its human writers 'spoke from God as they were carried along by the Holy Spirit' (2 Peter 1:21). In Dr J. I. Packer's vivid illustration, 'The Bible appears like a symphony orchestra, with the Holy Ghost as its Toscanini; each instrument has been brought willingly, spontaneously, creatively, to play his notes *just as the great conductor desired*, though none of them could ever hear the music as a whole.'[1]

While we do not have any of the Bible's original documents available to us today, I believe with the seventeenth-century Puritans not only that both Old and New Testaments were God-breathed, but that, by God's 'singular care and providence' they have been 'kept pure in all ages'. This brings us to the tingling truth that to pick up a Bible is to hold in one's hand nothing less than the living Word of the living God. I find that both awe-inspiring and exhilarating!

The second conviction I have is that Christians are meant to *enjoy* the Bible. John Calvin rightly describes the Bible as 'the sceptre by which the heavenly King rules his people', but this does not mean that we are to look upon it as a rod of iron. Nor, on the other hand, is it to be treated trivially as some kind of religious toy, to be used for our spiritual entertainment. Instead, it is meant to be a constant means of enlightenment, enrichment and encouragement, its dynamic influence bringing a deepening joy into our daily lives.

Sadly, many Christians seem to fall short of that experience. They read the Bible, perhaps regularly, but if they were to be absolutely honest about their reading they would have to confess that the whole business has become a duty rather than a delight. Others have got into a rut over the method they use for studying the Bible, with the result that they, too, are becoming bored rather than blessed. I dearly hope that this book will be a help to people who find themselves in situations like these. However, it is not basically meant to be a rescue operation. It is written by an ordinary Christian to other ordinary Christians, explaining very simply from my own study and experience why and how we *can* enjoy the Bible, and find it to be a daily source of spiritual power.

In the late nineteen-forties the late Rev. G. R. Harding Wood wrote a delightful little book entitled *Enjoy your Bible*. After his death, Mrs Maureen Vellacott, Mr Wood's beneficiary, kindly gave me permission to use the same title for an entirely new work which was published in 1978. This present volume is a considerably revised edition of the 1978 publication and is now presented under a new title.

I would like to express my thanks to Mrs Joy Hills, who typed the manuscript with the same efficiency as she does other secretarial work for me. My prayer is that many Christians will receive as much genuine help and enjoyment from reading this book as I did in writing it.

JOHN BLANCHARD
Banstead
Surrey

March 1984

1.
The truth behind the title

'Enjoy your Bible.' To almost everybody outside of the Christian church, and to not a few inside it, those words constitute at worst an absurdity, and at best a mild contradiction in terms. To many non-Christians, and especially to those with no particular religious beliefs, the Bible is no more than an antiquated collection of myths and fables. To others, it seems to be some kind of moral rulebook, and a rather forbidding one at that. Others will regard it as no more than a jumbled collection of men's religious thoughts, while some might be prepared to concede that, like the proverbial curate's egg, it is good in parts.

To be perfectly realistic, these reactions are quite predictable; we should expect unbelievers to think like that. The greater tragedy is when professing Christians, while presumably approaching the Bible with greater piety, seem to do so with little more pleasure. For many of them, the Bible is something they seem to endure rather than enjoy. They appear to recognize that in some mysterious way the Bible is 'God's book', but feel that a conglomeration of history, morals and ethics hardly seems likely to make them jump for joy! Then why the title *How To Enjoy Your Bible*?

The Bible's own people

My first answer to the question would be that that is precisely what certain people in the Bible did! One writer alone says of God's Word, 'I *rejoice* in following your statutes as one rejoices in great riches' (Psalm 119:14); 'I *delight* in your commandments because I love them'

(Psalm 119:47); 'I *delight* in your law' (Psalm 119:70) and 'I *rejoice* in your promise like one who finds great spoil' (Psalm 119:162). Even Jeremiah, sometimes called 'the weeping prophet' because of the solemn message he was called to deliver, could cry to God, 'When your words came I ate them; they were my *joy* and my heart's *delight*' (Jeremiah 15:16). The Christmas message, central to the whole Bible, was said by the angel who brought it to be 'good news of great *joy*' (Luke 2:10), while Paul's readers at Thessalonica welcomed God's Word 'with the *joy* given by the Holy Spirit' (1 Thessalonians 1:6). For all of these people, and for many others, the Word of God was a source of great rejoicing; it was something to be enjoyed.

But why did it, and should it, have this kind of impact, and produce this kind of response? It is certainly not because the Bible consists of nothing but niceties, a collection of compliments, comforts and congratulations. While it does contain many matchless words of joy, hope, love and peace, it also makes costly demands, imposes firm disciplines and hammers home some truths that hurt a great deal. Take those passages that expose our sin, unbelief, compromise and pride, for instance. What joy can we possibly get from reading those? What pleasure can there be in having those things applied to our lives? The answer comes in passages like these: 'Know then in your heart that as a man disciplines his son, so the Lord your God disciplines you' (Deuteronomy 8:5); 'My son, do not despise the Lord's discipline and do not resent his rebuke, because the Lord disciplines those he loves, as a father the son he delights in' (Proverbs 3:11, 12). As Christians, we should be grateful that God's Word does not allow our lives to go unchecked, unchallenged, unchastened, and the more mature we become, the more grateful we shall be for this. God rebukes us in order to restore us and hurts in order to heal. It is precisely for this reason that one of the Old Testament writers is able to say, 'Blessed is the man whom God corrects; so do not despise the discipline of the Almighty. For he wounds, but he also binds up; he injures, but his hands also heal' (Job 5:17, 18).

The Bible's own purpose

Yet this first answer to the question, 'Why enjoy your Bible?', is not the most important one. To say that to enjoy the Bible is *biblical* (because godly people in the Bible did so) and *sensible* (because even the 'hard' parts are written for our benefit) helps to drive us back to the best answer of all, which in turn is the answer to another more important question: 'Why was the Bible written in the first place?'

Reduced to its simplest possible terms, the Christian answer to that question can be put in the form of three statements:

1. The living, eternal, sovereign God, the creator and sustainer of the universe, is morally and spiritually so far removed from man that, left to himself, man could never come to know him.

2. If man is to know God, and if God and man are to come together in a living, harmonious relationship, then God must reveal himself to man; he must take the initiative, draw back the curtain, bridge the gap, break the silence, start the conversation. As someone has put it, 'Our need of revelation is *total*.' We can know nothing whatever about God unless God chooses to reveal himself to us.

3. God has done precisely that. He has done so *generally* in creation, so that the visible world around us testifies to the power and majesty of its Creator; and he has done so *specially* by means of the Bible. We shall see later on how insistent the Bible is on this point, but for the moment let us just put two of its statements side by side. The first is the apostle Paul's declaration that 'All Scripture is God-breathed' (2 Timothy 3:16). The second is the assertion of the writer of Hebrews that 'In the past God spoke to our forefathers through the prophets at many times and in various ways' (Hebrews 1:1). Taken together, these two tremendous statements tell us that the God who would otherwise be unknowable has made himself known by word of mouth. God has spoken to us, and done so in a personal, understandable way.

But *why*? What is his purpose in speaking to us? In his excellent little book *God Has Spoken,* Dr J. I. Packer gives this superb reply: 'The truly staggering answer which the Bible gives to this question is that God's purpose in revelation *is to make friends with us.* It was to this end that he created us rational beings, bearing his image, able to think and hear and speak and love; he wanted there to be genuine personal affection and friendship, two-sided, between himself and us – a relationship not like that between a man and his dog, but like that of a father to his son, or a husband to his wife. Loving friendship between two persons has no ulterior motive; it is an end in itself. And this is God's end in revelation. He speaks to us simply to fulfil the purpose for which we were made; that is, to bring into being a relationship in which he is a friend to us, and we to him, he finding his joy in giving us gifts and we finding ours in giving him thanks.'

Perhaps we should be careful to add here that this is in no way to suggest that God *needed* human friendship. He did not create man and then communicate with him in order to satisfy his own loneliness; after all, there is eternal fellowship with the triune Godhead of Father, Son and Holy Spirit. God is magnificently and uniquely self-sufficient and independent. Nevertheless, Packer's comment beautifully brings out God's purpose in revealing himself to man through his written Word.

But that is still not the whole story, because not only is the Christian answer based on the Bible, it is centred in Christ. We can begin to see this, for instance, by completing the last two biblical quotations we have used. The writer to the Hebrews, while making it clear that there were times when God had chosen to reveal himself through the prophets, adds, 'But in these last days he has spoken to us by his Son,' while Paul also tells Timothy that a man is made wise for salvation 'through faith in Christ Jesus'. In other words, God's fullest revelation of himself is not in print nor in precepts, but in person. As the apostle John puts it, 'The Word [that is, Jesus] became flesh and lived for a while among us. We have seen his glory, the glory of the one and only Son, who came from the Father, full of grace and truth' (John 1:14). Every part of the Bible points to Jesus, and when the picture is complete we see him not only as the Revealer, but as the Redeemer, not only *showing* man the way to a right relationship with God, but *providing* it. As we have already seen, man's great need is the life which comes from knowing God; but that need can only be met in Jesus Christ, who said, 'I am the way and the truth and the life. No one comes to the Father except through me' (John 14:6). As the whole Bible, from Genesis to Revelation, points us to the one who provides such a complete answer to our spiritual need, surely we should *enjoy* the message it has for us?

The Bible's own pictures

The story is told of an occasion when Queen Victoria was visiting a village somewhere in England. It was customary for church bells to be rung when royalty paid such a visit, but on this occasion none were to be heard. Angry at what he thought to be a slight on the queen, an official demanded a reason from one of the local dignitaries. 'Sir', the man replied, 'I can give you ten reasons why the bells were not rung. The first is that we do not have any bells ...' 'That will do,' the official interrupted, 'I don't need to know the other nine'! In this introductory chapter, we have been answering the question, 'Why enjoy your Bible?', and have concentrated on the major and most important

answer, which is that the Bible is God's Word to man,
revealing his own divine nature and character, inviting
alienated man back into a living relationship with him
and showing us his own provision of that way back in the
person of Jesus Christ. Having discovered that, there is a
sense in which we need no further answers to the question.
That one great truth covers everything. Yet it might be
helpful to round off the chapter by noting some of the
pictures the Bible uses to describe itself, because they
touch on so many of man's felt needs, and give us some
fascinating insights into the way in which the Bible can be
such a positive and powerful influence in our daily lives.
Here are nine, chosen at random.

Left to himself, man is morally and spiritually bankrupt;
the Bible is a *treasure*, 'more precious than gold, than
much pure gold' (Psalm 19:10).

Without God's voice, man is woefully ignorant; the
Bible is a *book of wisdom*, so that the psalmist is able to
say, 'I gain understanding from [God's] precepts' (Psalm
119:104).

Left to himself, man stumbles in moral and spiritual
darkness; the Bible is a *searchlight*, the same writer declaring, '[God's] word is a lamp to my feet and a light for my
path' (Psalm 119:105).

Man lives in an uncertain world; the Bible is a *guidebook*.
David acknowledges that 'All the ways of the Lord are
loving and faithful for those who keep the demands of his
covenant' (Psalm 25:10).

Man needs to know himself if he is to make stable progress in life; the Bible is a *mirror*, and man is told that if
he 'looks intently' into it, and acts wisely on what he
sees, 'he will be blessed' (James 1:25).

Man is basically restless and unsettled; the Bible is a
great *stabilizer*, and we are told of those who love God's
law that 'Nothing can make them stumble' (Psalm 119:
165).

Man is surrounded by temptation and constantly prone

to sin; the Bible is a great *purifier*, and speaks of 'washing with water through the word' (Ephesians 5:26).

Man lives in a world of rapidly changing and contrary opinions; the Bible is a *fixed point of reference*, so that the psalmist is able to say, 'Your word, O Lord, is eternal; it stands firm in the heavens' (Psalm 119:89).

Man is engaged in a lifelong battle against sin; the Bible is a powerful *weapon*, which Paul refers to as 'the sword of the Spirit' (Ephesians 6:17).

Yet of all the pictures the Bible uses to describe itself, none is more natural and effective than that of *food*. Now food is essential, of course, not just to a man's success or strength, but to his very survival; and spiritually his need of sustenance is just as vital. Jesus made it crystal clear that 'Man does not live on bread alone, but on every word that comes from the mouth of God' (Matthew 4:4), and the Bible is that word, that food. *Peter likens it to milk*, and says that we should drink it constantly, 'so that you may grow up in your salvation' (1 Peter 2:2). *Amos likens it to bread*, forecasting a time when there would be a famine, 'not a famine of food or a thirst for water, but a famine of hearing the words of the Lord' (Amos 8:11). *Ezekiel likens it to honey,* and says that when the word of God came to him 'it tasted as sweet as honey in my mouth' (Ezekiel 3:3).

What an amazing picture has emerged! Here is a book uniquely claiming to be God-breathed, bearing an invitation to eternal life, pointing out the answers to all of man's spiritual needs, and likening itself to an unrationed supply of the most nutritious foods ever discovered. And as if that were not enough, Isaiah flings its pages wide open and shouts, 'Come, all you who are thirsty, come to the waters; and you who have no money, come, buy and eat! Come, buy wine and milk without money and without cost' (Isaiah 55:1).

You could hardly receive a more enthusiastic invitation to enjoy your Bible!

2.
Countering the critics

So far, so good. The Bible lies open before us, making tremendous claims on its own behalf and promising untold blessing for those who read it diligently and follow it carefully. But is the issue really as straightforward as that? Not quite! While it is true that the Bible has legions of supporters — it is now printed in more editions, rendered in more versions, translated into more languages and sold in more millions of copies than ever before in its long history — it also has a dogged army of critics, those who for one reason or another would refuse to accept the statements we have made so far. Now there are two ways of responding to criticism of this kind: one is to ignore it, and the other is to examine it carefully, to see whether it is valid. In other words, you can either shut your ears or open your eyes! Some Christians might protest that that is being much too accommodating, but I am trying to be as fair as possible, and at the same time to be of the maximum help to those on the fringes of getting to grips with the Bible, either as young Christians or as those genuinely seeking to know whether it can be trusted. For them, it is not enough to suggest that they fling a handful of texts at the opposition, then put their hands over their ears. If someone is invited to enjoy his Bible, he will surely want to examine the claims of those who suggest that the food has been poisoned!

For the reader interested in pursuing this particular

line of study in detail, there are many excellent books available on the subject. One of the most readable is *Nothing but the Truth* by Brian Edwards. Here we must settle for a very brief and general look at some of those who oppose the Bible's own teaching about itself.

Those who deny its authority

For many of the Bible's critics, the word 'modern' seems to be the most important in the whole world. They claim that their position is based on modern scholarship, modern interpretations, modern discoveries, modern methods of research, and so on. The implication is clear: in recent times (say something like the last 200 years) man has developed and exercised his faculties to such a pitch that he is now able to pronounce on the authority — in other words the essential authorship — of the Bible in a way beyond the ability of his benighted forefathers. That seems to be mildly arrogant, to say the least!

In point of fact, the very first Bible critic to cast doubt on its authority did so before a single word of it had been written, and before its first human writer was even born! In Genesis 2:16, 17 God told Adam and Eve the very clear conditions under which they were to live in the Garden of Eden, but just a few sentences later we read that the devil, mysteriously appearing in the form of a serpent, came to Eve with the taunting question: 'Did God really say . . .?' (Genesis 3:1). Notice the thrust of the question. At a time when the sum total of the recorded words spoken directly by God to man would have occupied less than a minute, the devil denied their authority. He has not lacked followers. As A. W. Pink has rightly commented, 'Every effort that is being made to deny the Divine inspiration of the Scriptures, every attempt put forward to set aside their absolute authority, every attack on the Bible which we now witness in the name of scholarship, is only a repetition of this ancient question.'[1] Casting doubt upon whether God has spoken, or whether he said what he meant, or meant what he said, is not as brilliantly modern a critical device as some people would seem to suggest!

Every part of the Bible has been under attack from this quarter, but the Old Testament has been the primary target. Yet the critic who attempts this wholesale assault is up against massive problems. The words 'God said', 'God spoke', 'The word of the Lord came', and so on occur nearly 4,000 times in the Old Testament, 700 times in the first five books alone, forty times in one chapter. And what about Paul's assertion that *all* of these Old Testament writings were 'God-breathed' (2 Timothy 3:16), and Peter's statement that their human writers were not recording their own views and opinions, but that they 'spoke from God as they were carried along by the Holy Spirit'? (2 Peter 1:21.) The man who sets out to make a blanket attack on the authority of the Bible will find himself outgunned very early on in the action.

Those who deride its simplicity

By this I mean those who would claim that in one way or another, 'Science has disproved the Bible.' Again, the inference is clear: the Bible is believable only by those who will not accept allegedly 'superior' scientific facts. But is that a fair, *honest* argument? I can immediately think of at least six reasons why it is not.

Firstly, while the facts it records in these areas are accurate, the Bible is not a textbook on any of the natural sciences, and is therefore not open to criticism because it fails to develop these subjects. For instance, while it mentions stars, rocks and animals, it is not a research manual on astronomy, geology or biology. Nor, for that matter, does it tell us the depth of the Dead Sea, the temperature at which water boils, or the average weight of a fully grown duck-billed platypus! Those things are irrelevant to its purpose. Its great concern is with God and man and their relationship to each other, and when it deals with man it majors on his conduct, not on his chromosomes.

Secondly, the Bible often uses figures of speech such as allegories, parables, metaphors, symbols and similes, and their place and meaning must be understood correctly before any honest attempt to 'disprove' them can even get under way. To give just one example, the Bible begins to describe a global catastrophe with the words, 'The floodgates of the heavens were opened' (Genesis 7:11). Now it would be as ridiculous for a scientist to refute that statement on the grounds that there was no such apparatus in the stratosphere as it would be for us to suggest that God was guilty of cruelty to animals when a friend told us that in his part of the country it was 'raining cats and dogs'!

Thirdly, even when they observe the facts, scientists are not infallible, and sometimes draw the wrong conclusions. There is a story of a professor of zoology conducting experiments using a performing flea. After making the little fellow hop around on his arm for a while, he pulled the creature's legs off, and then shouted, 'Jump!' When the flea remained still, the professor beamed at a colleague and announced, 'There – I have just proved that when I remove a flea's legs it goes deaf!' The story is presumably apocryphal, but the same kind of error has often been made in interpreting what the Bible says.

Fourthly, scientific 'knowledge' is constantly developing, and sometimes has to change direction in order to do so. In 1861, the renowned French Academy of Science issued a booklet listing fifty-one 'scientifically proven facts' which contradicted the Bible. Today, our scientists no longer accept a single one of those 'facts'. In true science, humility is never out of place!

Fifthly, science provides no answers to man's greatest problems. It cannot remove his guilt, pardon his sin, cleanse his desires or remove his fear of death — issues on which the Bible majors. In the words of psychologist Paul Tournier, 'Everybody today is searching for an answer to those problems to which science pays no attention.'

Sixthly, between true scientific discovery and a true understanding of what the Bible says, there is in fact no conflict. Researched truth and revealed truth are friends, not enemies. As Lord Rayleigh, the Nobel prize-winning physicist put it, 'In my opinion, true science and true religion neither are nor could be opposed.' Many of the world's greatest scientists, past and present, have been convinced Bible believers. Sir Isaac Newton, who discovered both the calculus and universal motion, and is considered by some to have been the greatest scientific genius of all time, once said, 'I count the Scriptures of God to be the most sublime philosophy.' Michael Faraday, the brilliant pioneer of electrical science, believed the Bible to be the Word of God. Sir Ambrose Fleming, whose discoveries gave radio to the world, held firmly to the authority and inspiration of the Scriptures. So did Sir James Simpson, who pioneered the use of chloroform in surgery. Today, thousands of scientists across the world profess their faith in the Scriptures as the Word of God, and oppose with honest conviction the suggestion that science has disproved the Bible. That in itself does not clinch the case, of course; but neither can anyone say that science has *disproved* the Bible unless he can demonstrate that all of these scientific witnesses are deceived or dishonest.

Those who denounce its history

Another favourite line of attack is the one which suggests

that the Bible is hopelessly at fault as to the date when the earth came into being. One of the chief contributory factors to the continuing argument is that in the seventeenth century an Irish archbishop, James Ussher, in an attempt to reconstruct biblical chronology, came to the conclusion that the world was created in the year 4004 B.C. John Lightfoot, at one time Vice-Chancellor of Cambridge University, went even further, and claimed that creation took place during the week 18–24 October in that year, Adam himself having been created at 9 a.m. (Mesopotamian time) on the Friday of that week. Someone later commented that as a careful scholar, Lightfoot was doubtless unwilling to commit himself any further than that!

The fact that Ussher and Lightfoot were prominent churchmen may seem to make the Bible's case wobble a bit, but the real picture emerges when two key factors are taken into consideration. The first is that the scientists are by no means agreed in their own estimates of the earth's age. To test this, I have just turned to the first six textbooks on the subject that came to hand. In these, I find the age of the earth put at 3,400 million years, 4,500 million years, 4,600 million years, 4,750 million years, 10,000 million years and 12,000 million years – hardly unanimous! The second key factor is that the Bible makes *no mention of a date* for the origin of the earth. This means, of course, that the whole supposed argument between science and the Bible on the question of the earth's age should be declared 'No Contest'. There is no conflict between Genesis and geology. All we can say for certain on this particular issue is that whereas not all the different dates suggested by science can possibly be right, the Bible, by its silence on the subject, cannot possibly be wrong! And the Bible contents itself with the matchlessly simple words: 'In the beginning God created the heavens and the earth' (Genesis 1:1).

Those who decry its accuracy

Put very simply, this attack suggests that as we can no
longer lay our hands on any of the original manuscripts,
there must always be doubt as to the accuracy of the
writings we have collected together and called 'the Bible'.
Some would even say that the area of doubt is so large
that we would be safer to reject them all. But is this the
case? In other words, can we trust the text?

Some fascinating work has been done in this field, and
some of its results can be summarized by answering two
questions about our available manuscripts and the original
words which gave rise to the contents of our present Bible.
In doing so, we shall relate the same answers to other
ancient historical works whose accuracy is generally
accepted without question. What do the experts have to
tell us?

1. What copies do we have?

Of Caesar's *Gallic War* we have nine or ten good manuscript copies; of the *History* of Herodotus, about eight;
of the writings of Thucydides, eight manuscripts and a few
papyrus scraps, and of the *History* of Tacitus (who lived
at the close of the New Testament era) just two. And what
about the Bible? Taking the Old Testament first, the
famous Dead Sea Scrolls, discovered in a cave in Israel in
1947, consist of about 40,000 fragments, and make up
more than 500 copies of various books. For the New Testament we have some 5,250 manuscripts in the original Greek
text (to say nothing of over 86,000 very early Latin, Syrian
and Egyptian translations). A staggering difference, to say
the least! It is no wonder that Sir Frederic Kenyon, one-
time Director of the British Museum, could write, 'The
number of manuscripts of the New Testament, of early
translations from it, and of quotations from it in the
oldest writers of the church, is so large that it is practically

certain that the true reading of every doubtful passage is
preserved in some one or other of these ancient authorities.
This can be said of no other ancient book in the world.'

2. How close can we get?

In other words, how close in time are the manuscripts
we have to the dates of the originals? To begin with the
same secular examples, in the case of Caesar's *Gallic War*,
about 1,000 years; the writings of Herodotus and Thucydides, over 1,300 years; and the *History* of Tacitus, at
least 700 years. What about the Bible? The Dead Sea
Scrolls (which incidentally give us a Hebrew text of all but
one of the thirty-nine Old Testament books) take us back
to the second century B.C., within about 200 years of some
of the originals. For the New Testament, the most important mass of manuscripts is from the fourth and fifth centuries, others are from the third century and a whole
collection of them come from about the year A.D. 200.
Finally, in the John Rylands Library, Manchester, there
is a manuscript of part of the Gospel of John dated some
time before A.D. 150 – only fifty years after the original.

Again the Bible's answers to its critics are very impressive, and even more so when we start comparing these
manuscripts with each other. The area of agreement is so
amazing, even in hand-copied documents separated from
each other by over 1,000 years, that Professor F. J. A.
Hort, the outstanding nineteenth-century Greek scholar,
could write that 'The amount of what can in any sense
be called substantial variation . . . can hardly form more
than a thousandth part of the whole text.'[2] To that extraordinary testimony, Sir Frederic Kenyon adds, 'The
Christian can take the whole Bible in his hand and say
without fear or hesitation that he holds in it the true
Word of God, handed down without essential loss from
generation to generation throughout the centuries.'[3]

Those who denigrate its integrity

The examination of any ancient book includes what used
to be called 'higher criticism'. Included in this is the
question of authorship, and some Bible critics have
suggested that they have found some large loopholes
here. They claim that the authors of individual books of
the Bible are not as stated or traditionally accepted. These
critics have been very active, but have they been successful? From the numerous cases that could be examined,
let us look at just two.

1. Moses and the Pentateuch

Elsewhere in the Old Testament, and again in the New
Testament, the Pentateuch (the first five books in the
Bible) is said to have been written by Moses, the great
Jewish lawgiver. Even Jesus, when quoting from Exodus,
referred to it as 'the book of Moses' (Mark 12:26). Not-
withstanding, critics have suggested that Moses could not
possibly have been the author of those books, because
writing was unknown in his day; he and his contemporaries
were illiterate, and the Pentateuch was hardly more than a
collection of religious folklore put together by unknown
authors hundreds of years after Moses' death. But the
facts will not fit. Archaeologists have discovered that
many hundreds of years before Moses was born, both
Egypt and Babylonia were 'full of schools and libraries'.
Assyriologist A. H. Sayce even goes so far as to say that
'The Babylonia of the age of Abraham [much earlier than
Moses] was a more highly educated country than the
England of George III'![4] Since we read in the Bible that,
'Moses was educated in all the wisdom of the Egyptians'
(Acts 7:22), it is hardly surprising to find Sayce comment-
ing, 'Moses not only could have written the Pentateuch,
but it would have been little short of a miracle had he not
been a scribe.'[5] Of all the liberal critics of the Pentateuch,

the best known have been the two nineteenth-century Hebrew scholars, K. H. Graf and Julius Wellhausen. Put very simply, their general theory was that, rather than being written by one basic author in the logical order in which we find them in the Bible, the books in the Pentateuch were a collection of at least four ancient documents rather shakily handed down from one generation to another, and finally cobbled together by an anonymous editor centuries after the time of Moses. Graf, Wellhausen and others, who developed this so-called 'documentary theory' even further, based their suppositions on such things as the variety of names used to define God, differences in language and style and duplicated accounts of certain events. The whole theory caught on like wildfire, and by the turn of the century it was widely accepted as the only valid interpretation of the origin of the Pentateuch.

The 'Wellhausen hypothesis', as it is sometimes known, was certainly clever, but it has proved far from conclusive. Every one of the arguments in its favour has been so brilliantly countered by competent biblical scholars that it has been described as 'leaking in every seam'! Without going into technical details, there are two general points that can be made here. The first is to bear in mind that Graf and Wellhausen began their studies from a very biased position, namely a refusal to accept the possibility of miracles. This meant that rather than the Bible having to be *explained*, its own plain statements had to be *explained away*, which is quite another matter! No honest investigation can proceed on that kind of basis. The second point is that the burden of proof lies with the prosecution! The Bible proceeds on the basis that it is telling the truth; any charge that it is guilty of fraud must be backed up by evidence, not propped up by possibilities, and nothing in the documentary theory has yet dislodged the fact that, in the words of Dr G. C. Aalders, 'History knows nothing of any author other than Moses for this section of our Bible.'[6]

2. Daniel and the book of Daniel

Based on a straightforward reading of the Bible's own evidence, it has traditionally been accepted that the book of Daniel was written by a man of that name at a time when part of the Jewish nation was held in captivity in Babylonia, that is to say, in the sixth century B.C. The book is divided into two distinct halves: chapters 1–6 are historical and carefully describe specific events which took place in Babylonia at that time, while chapters 7–12 record extraordinary visions and predictions of future events. Most of the book is in Hebrew and the remainder (2:4 – 7:28) in Aramaic.

That is a very simple outline, but the book itself is far from simple, and in an attempt to unravel some of its difficulties, liberal critics have tried to show that it was written as late as the second century B.C. (that is, in the period between the Old and New Testaments) by an unknown author who used Daniel's name to give his work added authority. If they are right, the Old Testament will have been torpedoed below the water-line, because if this particular book is a fake, and its 'prophecies' no more than descriptions of events written after they had happened, how can we be sure that other Old Testament books are genuine and infallible? The issue is as serious as that, but have the critics proved their case? Here is the briefest summary of some of their main attacks, and of the answers that can be given.

Attack: In the ancient Hebrew Bible, the book of Daniel does not appear in the 'Prophets' section but among the 'Writings', showing that it was written after the time of the prophets. *Answer:* This book was placed with the Writings because Daniel was not *technically* a prophet, that is, a divinely appointed mediator between God and the

Jewish people. Rather, he was a statesman serving in a heathen court. He did, however, possess the *gift* of prophecy, so that the New Testament can legitimately refer to him as 'the prophet Daniel' (Matthew 24:15).

Attack: The book's so-called 'prophecies' are so accurate in their details of events that occurred during the second century B.C., when the Jews were being persecuted by Antiochus Epiphanes, that they must have been written at that time, probably to encourage the Jews to stand firm in the belief that God would eventually deliver them. *Answer:* Although this is a popular modern criticism, it is only a reworking of a poor and ancient argument. Over 1,700 years ago a pagan philosopher by the name of Porphyry, the author of a book called *Against the Christians,* put about the same theory, not because he had any evidence to support it, but because *he did not believe that prophecy was possible.* But surely that is a totally dishonest position to take? What is more, it requires us to believe that the harrassed Jews took this contemporary forgery, deliberately inserted it into their sacred writings as part of the Word of God, and then used it as a basis of encouragement and hope under persecution! But that is as ridiculous as the suggestion that the disciples stole the body of Jesus, hid it away somewhere, and then went out prepared to die for their belief in his resurrection! Not only that, but Jesus himself, in referring to the book of Daniel, confirmed both its authorship and the accuracy of its prophecies.

Attack: Daniel mentions a king by the name of 'Darius the Mede' (5:31, etc.) but as there is no mention of him to be found elsewhere this is obviously an error, and presumably an invention. *Answer:* By no means! In the first place, we can only say that no other mention of Darius has been found *so far.* The argument from silence is notoriously dangerous, and many an anti-biblical assumption has been knocked on the head by an archaeologist's spade! Secondly, many of the detailed facts stated in the book have been brilliantly vindicated by other evidence, and Daniel does tell us that Darius was the son of Ahasuerus, that he became ruler of the Chaldeans on the death of Belshazzar, and that he did so when he was about sixty-two years old. These are rather risky details to put into a piece of fiction!

Attack: There are three Greek words for musical instruments, 'zither', 'lyre' and 'harp' mentioned in Daniel 3:5, but no Jew living in Babylonia in the sixth century B.C. could possibly have known any Greek. *Answer:* Nonsense! There is now clear evidence that Greek culture had penetrated that far by that time; there were, in fact, Greek mercenaries in Nebuchadnezzar's Babylonian army.

Attack: The Hebrew and Aramaic in the book are not strictly those of the sixth century B.C. *Answer:* That is not true. The Hebrew used is similar to that of Ezekiel, who lived at that exact period.

In one form or another, the 'higher critics' have been with us for 2,000 years, but in spite of all their efforts, they have yet to demonstrate one conclusive crack in what W. E. Gladstone once called 'the impregnable rock of Holy Scripture'.

Those who doubt its credibility

This is the last group of critics we will have space to look at, and again we must simplify the argument. Put bluntly, these critics say, 'We cannot accept the Bible as true because of the miracles it records.' Now the first thing the Bible must do is to plead guilty to the charge! Both Old and New Testaments are shot through with miracles from beginning to end. Creation, the flood, the Egyptian plagues, the provision of manna in the wilderness, the sun and the moon standing still, sick people instantaneously healed, others raised from the dead, Jesus walking on the water, five thousand people fed with a few loaves and fish, the resurrection and ascension of Jesus — they are all there, and recorded as fact.

Then what is the answer to the critic who says that these things could not have happened? Must we examine every miracle in detail to see whether we can find any grounds for thinking that they might have been 'scientifically possible'? Not at all. The answer is to recognize that the Bible is first and foremost a book about *God*, and the real question therefore becomes 'Were they *divinely* possible?', and this, of course, is the whole crux of the matter. If there is no God, and Jesus was not divine, then the Bible's miracles must be explained away. But if the God of the Bible does exist, and Jesus was divine, then the miracles have neither to be explained away, *nor even explained*. They need only be accepted as they stand. The Bible does not teach that in miracles nature suddenly behaved erratically for some unknown reason, but that miracles are unusual events caused by God for a specific purpose, often to demonstrate a truth about himself.

This means that the real difficulty about accepting miracles has nothing to do with their number or nature. The problem lies not in the pages of Scripture, but in the hearts and minds of those who come to the Bible with their own prejudiced viewpoints as to the existence of the power of the God of whom the Bible speaks. In other words, the problem is not lack of evidence — it has often been pointed out that there is more evidence for the resurrection of Christ than for the Roman invasion of Britain — but lack of faith.

. In this chapter we have looked at just six groups of Bible critics. Of course, there are many others — those who say that the New Testament conflicts with the Old, those who claim that some of the apostles teach opposing doctrines, those who point to apparent contradictions in different accounts of the same events, those who assert that certain texts are inaccurate, and so on. Some of the arguments are very complex and, to be fair, not all of the answers are simple and straightforward. If you would like to take a closer look at these issues, or at the areas of opposition we have touched on very briefly, you will be able to get guidance on further reading material from your minister, a well-read Christian friend, or a Christian bookseller or publisher. There is ample evidence that the Bible has withstood all its critics in an astonishing way, so that millions of people all over the world can identify with this statement by Dr W. E. Sangster: 'The Christian feels that the tooth of time gnaws all books but the Bible. Nineteen centuries of experience have tested the book. It has passed through critical fires no other volume has suffered, and its spiritual truth has endured the flames and come out without so much as the *smell* of burning.' A modern American preacher has used more picturesque language, and suggested that a person trying to destroy the credibility of the Bible is to be compared to a gnat climbing up Everest and threatening to smash it to pieces by stamping its left hind leg! Nothing the critics have said need ever prevent you from enjoying your Bible!

3.
The excellence of the evidence — 1

When someone suggested to the great English preacher
C. H. Spurgeon that he should preach a sermon in defence
of the Bible, he replied, '*Defend* it? I would as soon defend
a lion. *Let it loose!*' That was his typically vivid way of
saying that the Bible gives such powerful and convincing
evidence for itself that it does not need any outside help
in fighting its case. To quote the title of Robert Horn's
excellent little book on the subject, the Bible is uniquely
The book that speaks for itself. Yet as soon as the Bible
begins to speak, countless other witnesses want to jump up
and confirm the evidence. What we want to do at this
point, therefore, is to ensure that everyone has a fair say,
but at the same time to preserve some kind of order in
the proceedings! This is how we shall do it: in this chapter,
we shall listen to the Bible speaking, almost without inter-
ruption, about its own origin; in the next chapter, as the
Bible gives other evidence, we shall allow additional witnesses to join in.

Whatever else may be said about the Bible, it can hardly
be accused (to use one of its own phrases) of hiding its
light under a bowl! Earlier on, we noticed the apostle Paul's
declaration that 'All Scripture is God-breathed', and the
other New Testament claim that 'God spoke . . . through
the prophets', but, as we shall now see, these are only
two spokesmen for many others who will give the same
testimony.

In picking up a book, one's first question will almost certainly be 'Who wrote it?' In the case of the Bible, there are two answers to the question. The first is to say that the Bible is not just one book, but a collection of books, sixty-six in all, written by over forty authors during a period of over 1,600 years. It was written on three continents, Asia, Africa and Europe, and in three languages, Hebrew, Greek and Aramaic. Its writers had vastly differing backgrounds and positions in life. They included politicians, soldiers, priests, fishermen, shepherds, a Jewish rabbi and a Gentile doctor. Yet in spite of this great variety, one of the most amazing things about the Bible is its essential *unity*. Although its writers deal with the most important questions that have ever occupied men's minds, and write on a great number of controversial subjects, they do so with a harmony and continuity that are unique in all literature. This in itself is a remarkable piece of evidence. After all, the Bible is not a straightforward document serialized by succeeding generations, one consciously taking over where the other left off. Seen in its various parts, it includes public records, history, poetry, prophecy, sermons, hymns, letters and miscellaneous other documents: yet, as Professor F. F. Bruce has written, 'For all that, the Bible is not simply an anthology; there is a unity which binds the whole together. An anthology is compiled by an anthologist; but no anthologist compiled the Bible.'

Then what is the source and secret of its unity, its harmony, its continuity? The answer to that question is the second answer to our first one, 'Who wrote it?', and this time the answer is simply to say, 'God did.' In other words, while the Bible had many human *writers*, it had one divine Author. In William Hendriksen's words, 'Though every word is truly the word of the human *author*, it is even more truly the Word of God.'[1] As we shall now go on to see, this is the *biblical* view of Scripture; it is *the Bible's own evidence about itself*, so dogmatically given that the apostle Peter can write, 'Above all, you must understand that no prophecy of Scripture came about by the prophet's own interpretation. For prophecy never had its origin in the will of man, but men spoke from God as they were carried along by the Holy Spirit' (2 Peter 1:20, 21). Let us listen to some of this 'internal evidence' in more detail.

The voice of the Old Testament

In an earlier chapter we saw that phrases like 'God said' and 'the word of the Lord came' occur nearly 4,000 times in the Old Testament, and that alone should surely be enough to make any open-minded reader sit up and take notice. Yet these claims become even more telling when we notice certain other things about them.

First of all, there was the *conviction* with which these words were written. Let us look at just two examples. The prophet Jeremiah begins his book by confessing that he had no wish to be a prophet. He considered himself useless as a public speaker, and in any case too young for the job. But he then goes on to say, 'Then the Lord reached out his hand and touched my mouth and said to me, "Now, I have put my words in your mouth"' (Jeremiah 1:9). Notice that phrase: '*my* words . . . *your* mouth'! No wonder he wrote under such tremendous pressure that later he cried out that God's Word was 'in my heart like a burning fire, shut up in my bones' (Jeremiah 20:9). He had an irresistible conviction that he was declaring God's Word.

From the first words of Jeremiah we turn to what are described as 'the last words of David' (2 Samuel 23:1), arguably the greatest figure in the pages of the Old Testament. What does he say of his ministry? With no indication that he is speaking other than the simple truth, he says, 'The Spirit of the Lord spoke through me; his word was on my tongue' (2 Samuel 23:2). Here is the same unqualified conviction that he is speaking God's words on his behalf. As Dr J. I. Packer puts it, 'The prophets' messages corresponded not to editorials in *The Times*, but to proclamations from Buckingham Palace.'[2]

Secondly, there was the great *courage* with which their words were spoken. Again, let us take just two examples. Think of Moses, facing up to the tyrannical Pharaoh of Egypt and demanding that he release the Hebrews from their centuries of slavery. How could Moses do such a thing when earlier he had run away from the Egyptian authorities? The answer lies in his opening words to the ruthless ruler: 'This is what the Lord, the God of Israel, says . . .' (Exodus 5:1). All of history turned on that fateful interview; the fact that one of the principal characters was a mere sheep-hand is explained only by the fact that his message was one that God had laid upon him and given him the strength to deliver. His courage lay in his commission.

Or take Amos, another herdsman, this time from the little town of Tekoa. Like a bolt from the blue, he stormed into Bethel, capital of Jeroboam II's rich but rotten northern kingdom of Israel, and denounced the idolatry, corruption, immorality and oppression on every hand. When ordered out of the country, he insisted on staying until he had prophesied the most appalling disasters, including the king's own death. Why? What was it that had suddenly got into him? Listen to his own explanation: 'I was neither a prophet nor a prophet's son, but I was a shepherd, and I also took care of sycamore fig-trees. But the Lord took me from tending the flock and said to me, "Go, prophesy to my people Israel"' (Amos 7:14, 15). As has been neatly said, 'With Amos it was not a case of turning prophet in order to earn his living; it was a case of leaving his living to act as a prophet.' Like Moses, his courage could only be explained in terms of his commission.

But there is a third, vital factor about the Old Testament evidence, and that is its *confirmation,* not only by the New Testament writers in general, but by Jesus in particular. The attitude of the New Testament writers is certainly impressive. They quoted directly from the Old Testament over 300 times (more than sixty times from Genesis alone) and always did so on the basis of its divinely inspired authorship. It has aptly been said that 'The apostles at once fell into the habit of citing texts from the prophets as utterances of God, or of the Holy Ghost.' Peter, for instance, quoted from Psalm 69 and Psalm 109, and said that in both of them '*the Holy Spirit* spoke . . . through the mouth of David' (Acts 1:16–20). Gathered together for worship, the disciples quoted Psalm 2 in one of their prayers, and did not hesitate to say to God that in these words, 'You spoke *by the Holy Spirit* through the mouth of your servant, our father David' (Acts 4:25). Paul and Barnabas introduced a quotation from Isaiah with the words: 'This is what the Lord has commanded us' (Acts 13:47). The writer to the Hebrews said, '*The Holy Spirit* ... testifies to us . . .' and then quoted direct from the words of Jeremiah (Hebrews 10:15–17). The apostles had no doubt in their minds that they could quote indiscriminately from anywhere in the Old Testament and know that they were quoting from Scriptures that were divinely inspired.

But the greatest and most direct confirmation of all comes from the lips of Jesus himself, and that confirmation could not possibly be more complete or convincing. In the first place (setting the example later followed by the apostles and disciples) he quoted frequently from the Old Testament, and in doing so said or implied that the original words were divinely inspired. For instance, he challenged the Sadducees, 'But about the resurrection of the dead – have you not read *what God said* to you . . .?' (Matthew

22:31) and proceeded to quote from the writings of Moses at Exodus 3:6. He tackled the Pharisees in the same way, telling them that by misconstruing the words Moses wrote at Exodus 20:12 and Deuteronomy 5:16 they '*nullify the word of God*' (Mark 7:10–13). Later on, he quoted Psalm 110 and said that David was 'speaking *by the Holy Spirit*' (Mark 12:36). Even more remarkably, he took a phrase from Genesis 2:24 which in the original is not directly attributed to God, and introduced it with the words: '. . . at the beginning *the Creator* "made them male and female", and said . . .' (Matthew 19:4, 5). There was even an occasion when an argument with the Jews turned on one particular word in Psalm 82:6. Without a moment's hesitation Jesus pinned them to it, and then reminded them of a principle they already accepted, namely that 'the Scripture cannot be broken' (John 10:35). What an amazing confirmation of the divine authority of the Old Testament writings when we hear Jesus nailing his opponents down to one word in the original text! No wonder J. C. Ryle, the first Bishop of Liverpool, commented, 'Few passages appear to me to prove so incontrovertibly the plenary inspiration and Divine authority of every word in the original text of the Bible.'[3]

Yet even this is only the beginning as far as Jesus' confirmation of the Old Testament is concerned. In our first chapter we saw that the Bible's message centred on the person and work of Christ, and we need to come back to this point now, because we see it vividly illustrated as we notice how often Jesus related the events of his own life directly to the prophecies made in the Old Testament. In the Sermon on the Mount he said, 'Do not think that I have come to abolish the Law or the Prophets; I have not come to abolish them but to fulfil them' (Matthew 5:17). After reading a passage from Isaiah in his own local synagogue at Nazareth, he added, 'Today this scripture is fulfilled in your hearing' (Luke 4:21). Teaching his disciples that they, like him, would face bitter opposition in the world, he said, 'This is to fulfil what is written in their Law: "They hated me without reason"' (John 15:25). At the Last Supper, he referred sadly to his imminent betrayal by Judas, and then said, 'But this is to fulfil the scripture: "He who shares my bread has lifted up his heel against me"' (John 13:18). When Peter tried to prevent his arrest in the Garden of Gethsemane, Jesus rebuked him and said that if necessary legions of angels would come to deliver him, and then added, 'But how then would the Scriptures be fulfilled that say it must happen in this way?' (Matthew 26:54.) Moments later, he taunted his opponents for not arresting him earlier, and added, 'But the Scriptures must be fulfilled' (Mark 14:49). Even after his death and resurrection, nothing had changed; there was exactly the same emphasis. Meeting with the terrified remnant of disciples, the very first thing he did after convincing them that he was indeed risen from the dead was to say to them, 'This is what I told you while I was still with you: Everything must be fulfilled that is written about me in the Law of Moses, the Prophets and the Psalms' (Luke 24:44).

These last words are particularly significant, because they list the three major divisions of the Hebrew Scriptures. By using this one simple phrase, Jesus indicated that there was no part of the Old Testament which was unrelated to him. He saw his birth, life, death, resurrection, ascension and second coming as being inextricably interwoven with those sacred writings, so that it was impossible to interpret them without him, or understand him without them. The Christian has one Bible, not two; worships one God, not two; knows one way of salvation, not two. The Bible refers to Jesus as 'the Word of God' (Revelation 19:13) and Jesus refers to the Old Testament as 'the word of God' (Mark 7:13). Nothing could more vividly confirm the Old Testament's divine origin, inspiration and authority than that!

The voice of the New Testament

It will be as well to remind ourselves at this point that we
are still listening to *the Bible's evidence about itself.* So far
we have heard from the Old Testament, its writers speaking with conviction and courage, and their words being
confirmed by the New Testament writers in general and by
Jesus in particular. Now we turn directly to the New Testament. What does it have to say for itself? What voices do
we hear as it speaks?

Fascinatingly enough, the first part of the evidence is, as
it were, spoken in Hebrew, because it comes in *the words of
the Old Testament prophets*! We have already heard Jesus
underlining the authority of the Old Testament, and showing that it was totally linked with his own life and ministry;
now notice how the apostles allowed the Old Testament
to authenticate both their actions and their teaching. On
the Day of Pentecost, which could in one sense be called
the birthday of the Christian church, the most fantastic
events took place in Jerusalem. Previously frightened out
of their wits, the apostles had a tremendous encounter with
the Holy Spirit, and as a result began preaching the gospel
openly and fearlessly for the first time since Christ's death.
What is more, God brought about such a miraculous pheno-
menon that crowds visiting the city from all over the world
heard what they were saying in their own native language.
Completely baffled, they suggested that the apostles must
be drunk (though I am not sure how that could have
explained what happened!). At this point Peter stood up
and said, 'These men are not drunk, as you suppose. It's
only nine in the morning! No, this is what was spoken by
the prophet Joel . . .' (Acts 2:15, 16). Notice that! While
later emphasizing that what was happening was an act of
God, he began by saying that it was an act of God *prophesied in the Old Testament Scriptures.* And what was so
specifically true in this incident was generally true in

everything that was to follow. We could perfectly well call this particular part of the New Testament not 'the Acts of the Apostles' but 'the Acts of the God of the Old Testament', for that is what the disciples themselves claimed those acts to be.

The same was true of their teaching. When Philip got into conversation with the Ethiopian government official who was on his way home from a visit to Jerusalem, and saw that he was reading from the prophet Isaiah, he 'began with that very passage of *Scripture* and told him the good news about Jesus' (Acts 8:35). When Paul wanted to convince the Jews living in Thessalonica that Jesus was the Christ, the Messiah, he 'went into the synagogue, and on three Sabbath days he reasoned with them from *the Scriptures,* explaining and proving that the Christ had to suffer and rise from the dead' (Acts 17:2,3). Later, when he preached to the Jews at Berea, 'they received the message with great eagerness' but also 'examined *the Scriptures* every day to see if what Paul said was true' (Acts 17:11). Incidentally, the evidence they found must have been pretty convincing, because 'many of the Jews believed, as did also a number of prominent Greek women and many Greek men' (Acts 17:12). This, then, is the first part of the evidence. The Old Testament not only speaks of the New Testament, it speaks *in* it and *for* it.

The next part of the evidence comes in *the words of Jesus.* Religious teachers were two a penny in New Testament times. Pharisees, Sadducees, scribes, rabbis (both professional and amateur!) and teachers of every kind bombarded the people with their religious ideas, and in particular with their own party line as to the precise meaning of the Old Testament writings. Then Jesus burst on the scene, and by the end of the Sermon on the Mount we are told that 'the crowds were amazed at his teaching, because he taught *as one who had authority*, and not as their teachers of the law' (Matthew 7:28, 29). Back in

his home town of Nazareth the crowds asked, 'Where did
this man get this wisdom . . .?' (Matthew 13:54). Even the
temple police, who had no doubt heard hordes of religious
teachers in the course of their duties, had to admit to their
superiors, 'No one ever spoke the way this man does' (John
7:46). His words possessed such obvious and unique power
that they demanded an explanation quite out of the
ordinary. The one Jesus gave was this: 'I do nothing on my
own but speak just what the Father has taught me' (John
8:28). Later he backed this up by saying, 'I did not speak
of my own accord, but the Father who sent me
commanded me what to say and how to say it . . . So
whatever I say is just what the Father has told me to
say' (John 12:49, 50). What did he mean? Was he merely
saying that he was a kind of honours graduate in theology,
and able to speak more authoritatively than others on
religious issues? Far from it, for on another occasion he
told the Jews, 'I am telling you *what I have seen in the
Father's presence*' (John 8:38) — in other words in heaven,
in eternity. When Jesus came to earth he brought his
teaching with him; he did not just pick it up as he went
along!

Even more stunning was the comment he made to the
argumentative Jews a few moments later. Chiding them
because they refused to believe his words, he said, 'If I am
telling the truth, why don't you believe me? He who
belongs to God hears *what God says*. The reason you do
not hear is that you do not belong to God' (John
8:46, 47). Nothing could be clearer than that devastating
comment. Christ's words are God's words; to hear him is
to hear God. His authority is absolute, because it is divine.

So much for the direct words of Jesus about his own
teaching; but what guarantee have we that they were
recorded correctly, or that the rest of the New Testament
was accurately recorded? Jesus himself supplies the answer.
Just before his death he made his disciples one of the most

crucial promises recorded in the Bible, and it is surely not without significance that he repeated it three times. At his last meal with them, he said, 'All this I have spoken while still with you. But the Counsellor, the Holy Spirit, whom the Father will send in my name, *will teach you all things and will remind you of everything I have said to you*' (John 14:25, 26). Moments later, he drove home the promise even more firmly and said, 'I have much more to say to you, more than you can now bear. But when he, the Spirit of truth, comes, *he will guide you into all truth*. He will not speak on his own; he will speak only what he hears, and he will tell you what is yet to come. He will bring glory to me by taking from what is mine and making it known to you' (John 16:12–14). What a staggering promise! Not only would the apostles remember the facts that had taken place and the words that had been spoken, they would understand their meaning as never before, and be able to convey facts, words and meaning to the whole world in a way that would give their words the divine authority implicit in Christ's promise. As the famous third-century theologian Origen once said, 'The promised enabling of the Holy Spirit guaranteed that the New Testament writers would be rendered incapable of error or lapse of memory.'

The final part of the evidence comes *in the words of the New Testament writers*. Did they have both the sense and the certainty that their teaching was divinely inspired, their words God-given? Let three spokesmen answer for them all. First into the witness-box is the apostle *Paul*, the most prolific of all the New Testament writers. How did he view his ministry? His evidence could hardly be clearer. He told the Galatians that he was 'an apostle – sent not from men nor by man, but by Jesus Christ and God the Father' (Galatians 1:1). He challenged the boastful Corinthians, 'If anybody thinks he is a prophet or spiritually gifted, let him acknowledge

that what I am writing to you is the Lord's command'
(1 Corinthians 14:37). (Notice the force of that! As Dr
Leon Morris has put it, 'Some of the Corinthians thought
they had spiritual discernment. Let them show it by recognizing inspiration when they saw it'.) In a happier context,
Paul rejoiced that when he had preached the gospel in
Thessalonica there had been those who had received his
message 'not as the word of men, but as it actually is, the
word of God' (1 Thessalonians 2:13). (Would any preacher
dare to say that of every word he preached today?) Later
in the same letter, he laid down very firm instructions
about sexual behaviour, and added that 'He who rejects
this instruction does not reject man but God . . .' (1 Thessalonians 4:8). Again, he was claiming to be nothing less
than God's mouthpiece, and that every part of his teaching was to be accepted without question as divinely
authoritative.

Next comes *Peter*. Did he share Paul's conviction? Yes
he did! In a letter written to remind his hearers of certain
fundamentals of the Christian faith, he urged them to
'recall the words spoken in the past by the holy prophets
and the command given by our Lord and Saviour through
your apostles' (2 Peter 3:2). That last phrase is the key —
the Lord gave the word of command; the apostles delivered
it. The authority was the king's, not the ambassador's.
Peter also made a particular point of endorsing Paul's
apostolic authority. After telling his readers that Paul had
written to them 'with the wisdom that God gave him',
he went on to say that some people had distorted his
words, 'as they do *the other Scriptures*' (2 Peter 3:15, 16).
Notice that very carefully! Peter treated Paul's words as
part of 'the Scriptures', the sacred Word of God.

Finally, we have *John*, another of the apostolic 'heavyweights'. He began the last book in the Bible by saying
that what he was about to write was nothing less than 'the
word of God and the testimony of Jesus Christ' (Revelation

1:2); and in almost his final phrase he reminded his readers that 'These words are trustworthy and true,' having been given to him by 'the Lord, the God of the spirits of the prophets' (Revelation 22:6). Beyond all shadow of doubt, these words bear the same meaning as those used by Paul and Peter: the human writer is claiming to record, without addition or subtraction, error or exaggeration, the words of Almighty God.

We must take a break. The court, if you like, must recess! What is the position so far? We invited the Bible to speak for itself and it has done so in no uncertain fashion. Anyone setting out to discredit the Bible has to begin by turning aside from everything we have heard in this chapter. As the great American scholar B.B. Warfield once said, to try to maintain that the Bible does not claim to be the Word of God is like trying to avoid an avalanche by dodging individual boulders. The thing is impossible. If you have a biblical view of the Scriptures, you have no such problem. Every single stone in the torrent of testimony we have heard will be yet another reason why you can enjoy your Bible!

4.
The excellence of the evidence — 2

It is not unusual, when working in schools or colleges (and other places, for that matter) to hear someone say, 'The Bible is a load of rubbish.' Sometimes the turn of phrase used is a little less delicate! Yet when I ask the critic to give some examples of this 'rubbish', there is either an embarrassed silence or a feeble rephrasing of some ancient argument which has been mortally wounded for years.

In the last chapter, we listened to the Bible giving evidence on the question of its origin, and the testimony we heard, far from being 'rubbish', had all the hallmarks of truth about it. The Old Testament writers, Jesus himself and the New Testament writers all claimed with self-conscious certainty that they were writing or speaking nothing less than God's Word. Now let us listen to some further evidence, this time covering other areas, all of which can be tested outside of the Bible's pages.

The voice of history

As we have already seen, the Bible is much more than a history book, and it is not merely written in historical terms. Details contained in its poetry, visions and allegories, for instance, are obviously not to be taken as historical events. Yet its pages do include a great deal of historical

data, recording names, places, dates and other details by
the hundred. But are they *correct*? That is obviously an
important question, because if we cannot trust its history,
how can we be sure of its theology? If a history book
insisted that the Battle of Hastings took place in 1157
and that Napoleon was Emperor of Norway and the father
of Adolf Hitler, I would be disinclined to depend upon it
for an accurate assessment of man's moral development
through the Middle Ages! How does the Bible rate in this
field?

I suppose the only way to give a *complete* answer to
that question would be to list every name, date and place
recorded in the Bible, and then to see how far they agree
with details taken from apparently reliable non-biblical
sources. Obviously we cannot do that here, but if we did
so, two facts would emerge: the 'agreed' list would be
surprisingly long, and it would be growing longer all the
time! Of course, many hundreds of facts have never been
disputed; nobody has denied that Capernaum was 'a town
in Galilee' (Luke 4:31), or that Bethany was (and is!)
'less than two miles from Jerusalem'! (John 11:18.) But the
real fascination comes when we match the results of
archaeological discovery with the statements in the Bible
that cannot be confirmed by a fifteen-day dash around
the Middle East. This is especially true when we begin to
realize the amazing amount of detailed information that
is increasingly being unearthed, each new discovery filling
in one more gap in our knowledge. To take just one
example, the margin of error in fixing dates as far back as
about 600 B.C., in the words of one authority, 'almost
never exceeds a year, and in some cases is reduced to a
week within a month, or even to nil'. Now the Bible
records a vast stream of names, dates, places, events and
customs: how does it stand up to the bulldozer, the spade,
the ultra-violet light and the microscope?

Remarkably well, according to experts in this field. On

the Old Testament, Professor W. F. Albright, the world's greatest orientalist, wrote in 1958, 'Thanks to modern research we now recognize [the Bible's] substantial historicity. The narratives of the patriarchs, of Moses and the exodus, of the conquest of Canaan, of the judges, the monarchy, exile and restoration, have all been confirmed and illustrated to an extent that I should have thought impossible forty years ago.'[1] In the New Testament, no writer has come under more constant attack than Luke, who wrote one of the Gospels and the Acts of the Apostles. At one time or another he has been accused of being at fault over dates, places, people and customs. Yet increasingly he is being proved completely dependable. To take just one example, Luke wrote that John the Baptist began his ministry 'in the fifteenth year of the reign of Tiberius Caesar — when Pontius Pilate was governor of Judea, Herod tetrarch of Galilee, his brother Philip tetrarch of Iturea and Trachonitis, and Lysanias tetrarch of Abilene . . .' (Luke 3:1). All the early details were checked, putting the date at about A.D. 27, but the only Lysanias who could be traced was one who died in 36 B.C. Was Luke wrong? If so, he was *very* wrong — the equivalent of saying that John F. Kennedy was President of the United States of America before the First World War! Then an inscription was found near Damascus which referred to 'Lysanias the Tetrarch' and was dated A.D. 14–29, proving Luke right after all.

Many other examples could be given, all pointing in the same direction. After exhaustive research, Sir William Ramsay, one of the world's most outstanding archaeologists, said that Luke 'should be placed along with the very greatest of historians'. The eminent Jewish archaeologist Nelson Glueck is on record as referring to 'the almost incredibly accurate historical memory of the Bible', and as saying, 'It may be stated categorically that no archaeological discovery has ever controverted a biblical reference.'[2] Archaeology can never prove the Bible's claim to be the Word of God; but what it can do, and is increasingly doing, is to show that its civil, social and religious history is amazingly dependable.

The voice of prophecy

It has sometimes been said that the Bible stakes its reputation on its prophecies, and that is by no means an exaggeration. But as soon as we come to the subject of prophecy we run up against the problem of false prophets, charlatans, cranks and con-men of one kind or another who have made the most fantastic statements, and claimed divine authority for doing so. Needless to say, they did not catch God unawares, and right back at the time when the law was given to Moses, God gave a very simple test that would immediately weed out most of these: 'If what a prophet proclaims in the name of the Lord does not take place or come true, that is a message the Lord has not spoken. The prophet has spoken presumptuously' (Deuteronomy 18:22). It is important to notice that those genuinely called to be prophets took that test seriously, and applied it literally. Many years later, when Micaiah prophesied the imminent death of King Ahab at the battle of Ramoth Gilead, the king gave orders for him to be flung into prison 'until I return safely' (1 Kings 22:27). Without flinching, Micaiah told him, 'If you ever return safely, the Lord has not spoken through me' (1 Kings 22:28). As the penalty for false prophecy was instant execution, Micaiah was literally staking his life on the fact that God had given him the words to speak. And what happened to Ahab? Although he went into battle disguised as an ordinary soldier, he could not avoid his God-appointed fate. One Syrian arrow, aimed nowhere in particular, homed in on the disguised king and found one small gap in his armour. By nightfall he was dead. When a prophet spoke in God's name, nothing could prevent the prophecy coming true.

The other, crucial test of prophecy (which incidentally included 'forth-telling' God's Word as well as 'foretelling' it) was that it would never conflict with the truth that God had already revealed through Moses, but would call those who heard it to 'follow [the Lord your God] . . . Keep his commands and obey him; serve him and hold fast to him' (Deuteronomy 13:1–5). In other words, the true prophet was a man of God, and therefore of God's Word. He was not just a religious fortune-teller. He did not dabble with crystal balls or tea leaves. His prophetic words came *direct from God*, the one who alone could say, 'I am God, and there is none like me. *I make known the end from the beginning*, from ancient times, what is still to come . . . What I have said, that will I bring about; what I have planned, that will I do' (Isaiah 46:9–11). This explains precisely why the words of the true prophet had the divine hallmarks of authority, purity and certainty.

To do anything like a full check on the Bible's prophecies would take volumes, not pages, but it is fascinating to take a look at even one or two examples from the Old Testament. About 920 B.C. an unnamed prophet told Jeroboam, the first King of Israel, that his throne would one day be occupied by a king called Josiah, who would sweep away the appalling idolatry that Jeroboam was promoting. Nearly 300 years later, when King Amon died, we read that 'Josiah his son succeeded him as king' and immediately began to carry out the precise programme of moral reformation which the prophet had predicted (compare 1 Kings 13:1, 2 with 2 Kings 21:25–22:2 and 2 Kings 23:15–18).

Then we have the writings of Isaiah, who prophesied for over forty years from about 740 B.C. In an extraordinary way, he predicted a whole series of future events, including the downfall of Jerusalem and the wholesale deportation of the Jews to Babylon. Then, even more remarkably, he prophesied that the end of their captivity would be brought about by someone called Cyrus, who would release the Jews for the specific purpose of rebuilding the temple at Jerusalem (see Isaiah 44:28). Exactly as forecast, the Babylonians sacked Jerusalem and took the Jews away captive. In 538 B.C., nearly 200 years after Isaiah's words, the pagan King of Persia conquered Babylon and, as one of his first acts, released all the foreigners the Babylonians had captured, with specific instructions to the Jews that they should 'go up to Jerusalem in Judah and build the temple of the Lord, the God of Israel' (see Ezra 1:1–3, where we are also told that this fulfilled a prophecy made by Jeremiah). And the king's name? *Cyrus*!

Examples like these are certainly remarkable, but they are only the tip of the prophetic iceberg. When we begin to add them all together, and check them with subsequent history, the whole thing becomes mind-boggling. To illustrate this, the American scientist Peter W. Stoner applied a mathematical calculation to just eleven of the hundreds of Old Testament prophecies later recorded as historically fulfilled. At the end of the day he found that the probability of these eleven predictions being fulfilled by chance was the same as that of a man successfully picking out one marked silver dollar from a pile so staggering in size that it could only be formed by accumulating a volume equivalent to that of 2 trillion galaxies, each containing 100 billion stars, every second for twenty-one years![3]

When we begin to consider the prophecies concerning the Messiah (the Hebrew word for Christ) both the details and the overall weight of the evidence are equally amazing. The prophets foretold that he would be born of a virgin (Isaiah 7:14) in the family line of Jesse (Isaiah 11:1) and the family of David (Jeremiah 23:5). They said that although he would perform miracles (Isaiah 32:1–4) and ride into Jerusalem in triumph on a donkey (Zechariah 9:9), he would be rejected by the Jews (Isaiah 53:3), betrayed (Psalm 41:9), pierced through hands and feet (Psalm 22:16), and put to death with law-breakers (Isaiah 53:12). Yet that would not be the end, for he would rise from the dead (Psalm 16:10) and ascend into heaven (Psalm 68:18). It is actually possible to sketch in virtually all the essential facts in the biography of Jesus from words all written over 400 years before he was born. Altogether, there are well over 100 Old Testament prophecies about Christ and someone has calculated that, according to the Law of Compound Probabilities, the odds against them being fulfilled in the life of one person are a staggering 6,451,144,325,125,601,253,342,971,930,704,920 to 1. That being accepted, we can hardly be accused of exaggerating when we say that the Bible's evidence shows it to be dependable!

The voice of society

Many centuries ago the psalmist wrote these words about the Scriptures: 'The law of the Lord is perfect, reviving the soul. The statutes of the Lord are trustworthy, making wise the simple. The precepts of the Lord are right, giving joy to the heart. The commands of the Lord are radiant, giving light to the eyes. The fear of the Lord is pure, enduring for ever. The ordinances of the Lord are sure and altogether righteous' (Psalm 19:7–9). When Jesus came, he put the same kind of language in the form of a promise and declared, 'I am the light of the world. Whoever follows me will never walk in darkness, but will have the light of life' (John 8:12). Those are very far-reaching claims, but has history borne them out? Has the Bible in general, and the teaching of Jesus in particular, had that kind of dynamic, revolutionary, cleansing effect? What impact has it made on society?

Those questions produce a crucial test, which we can illustrate very simply. Supposing I hand someone a packet labelled 'Antirrhinum Seeds', with a lovely picture of that flower on the cover. Being a suspicious type, he says, 'I don't believe these are antirrhinum seeds. What proof can you give me?' The question is perfectly fair, and the answer equally obvious: let him plant the seeds and watch the results! Now the Bible claims that its teaching has the power to change men's lives, revolutionize them for the better. Using the very analogy of sowing and growing, Paul says that 'The fruit of the Spirit is love, joy, peace, patience, kindness, goodness, faithfulness, gentleness and self-control' (Galatians 5:22, 23). That is what is written on the packet; what has come up where the seed has been sown? Some years ago, *Reader's Digest* carried an amazing story called 'Shimabuku – The Village that lives by the Bible'. When American troops liberated Okinawa towards the end of World War II, they found it in an appalling social and moral condition. Then they reached the village of Shimabuku, where they were greeted by two old men, one of them carrying a Bible. Suspicious of a trap, they entered the village very cautiously – only to find it spotlessly clean, its fields tilled and fertile, and everything a model of neatness and cleanliness, in stark contrast to all the other villages round about. The reason? Thirty years earlier an American missionary, on his way to Japan, had called at Shimabuku. He only stayed long enough to make two converts (those two old men), teach them some hymns, leave them a Japanese translation of the Bible, and urge them to live by it. With no other Christian contact, and guided only by that Bible, those two men had transformed their community. There was no jail, no brothel, no drunkenness, no divorce; instead, the people lived healthy, happy, fulfilled lives – an oasis of love and purity in a desert of degradation all around them. Clarence Hall, the war correspondent who wrote the story, summed up his feelings in the words of his dumbfounded driver: 'So this is what comes out of only a Bible and a couple of old men who wanted to live like Jesus! Maybe we're using the wrong kind of weapons to change the world.'

While there have certainly been men who have twisted the Bible's teaching to their own evil ends, and others who have wrongly claimed biblical warrant for many kinds of injustice and oppression, the evidence of history is that wherever the straightforward teaching of the Bible has been rightly applied and obeyed, society has undergone a moral and spiritual revolution. The eighteenth-century German philosopher Immanuel Kant, who denied that God could be known in a personal way, nevertheless admitted, 'The Bible is an inexhaustible fountain of all truths' and, 'The existence of the Bible is the greatest blessing which humanity ever experienced.' James Russell Lowell, one-time American ambassador in England, challenged anyone to find a place on the face of the earth, ten miles square, where a man could live in decency, comfort and security, supporting and educating his children, unspoiled and unpolluted; a place where age is reverenced, infancy respected, womanhood honoured and human life held in due regard, where the gospel of Christ had not cleared the way, laid the foundations and made decency and security possible. The challenge was never accepted; nor could it be accepted today. The sheer moral power of the Bible is beyond question, and to the Christian that power has only one explanation.

The voice of Deity

In these two chapters we have looked at some of the evidence in the Bible's favour. Some of it has been internal, some external; it has come from its writers and its readers; it has had the support of prophecy and history; it has been backed up by careful learning and changed living. The combined weight of it all would seem to be utterly overwhelming. Yet, in spite of it all, the vast majority of people reject the Bible's claims and therefore its authority in their own lives. Why is this?

The Bible's answer to that question is clear and concise. The apostle Paul tells us that 'The man without the Spirit does not accept the things that come from the Spirit of God, for they are foolishness to him and he cannot understand them, because they are spiritually discerned' (1 Corinthians 2:14). The ultimate reason for rejecting the Bible – and, by implication, the ultimate evidence for accepting it – are locked into that one sentence. To take the negative point first, why does a man deliberately fly in the face of all the evidence and refuse to accept the divine inspiration of the Bible? Is it because he is not clever enough, or the Bible not clear enough? Not at all. It is because he is 'without the Spirit'. Just as men would have been unable to write the Bible without the Holy Spirit, so men are unable either to 'accept' or 'understand' it unless the Holy Spirit enables them to do so. They may agree that it is socially useful or morally helpful; they may acknowledge it is good literature or fine prose; but unless God himself opens their eyes to the fact, they will never bow to the doctrine that it is the inspired Word of God. The real trouble, in other words, is spiritual blindness, and in his second letter to the Corinthians, Paul tells us both the cause and the effect of this appalling disease: 'The god of this age [that is, the devil] has blinded the minds of unbelievers, so that they cannot see the light of the gospel of the glory of Christ, who is the image of God' (2 Corinthians 4:4).

But the same verse that gives the basic reason why men reject the Bible also points us to the ultimate reason why Christians accept it, and that is what the old theologians used to call 'the internal witness of the Holy Spirit'. To

put it as simply as possible, only the God who committed
its truth to those who wrote the Bible can confirm its
truth to those who read it. At the end of the day, only
God is capable of identifying his own handwriting!

It has been said that a man with an experience is never
at the mercy of a man with an argument. This is precisely
true here, as we can illustrate from the New Testament.
On one occasion, Jesus healed a man who had been born
blind. Needless to say, this caused a sensation, and when
the Pharisees found out that the miracle had taken place
on the sabbath, it blew up into a first-class storm, as they
believed that this broke the law of God. Time and again
they interrogated the man concerned: Where was Jesus
now? How had he healed him? What did he think of Jesus?
Didn't he know Jesus was a sinner? Eventually the man
could stand it no longer. Brushing aside the religious
question as to whether Jesus was a sinner by healing on
the sabbath, he told the Pharisees, *'One thing I do know:
I was blind but now I see!'* (John 9:25). That is exactly
the position of the genuine Christian believer with regard
to the Bible. Once he was blind as to its divine inspiration;
now he can 'see' — he knows beyond a shadow of a doubt
that the Bible is the Word of God. Nor is this just 'a funny
feeling', or wishful thinking; it is a deep, unshakeable,
supernatural conviction that only God can give. The great
German Reformer Martin Luther once wrote, 'The Holy
Spirit is no sceptic, and the things he has written in our
hearts are not doubts or opinions, but assertions — surer
and more certain than sense or life itself.'

To the unbeliever, that kind of statement is piffle, but
to the true Christian it is *powerful*, because he recognizes
it as part of his own living experience. He knows that his
inner conviction that the Bible is the Word of God is not
something he aimed at achieving, or worked out for
himself, nor is it the result of some kind of religious brain-
washing. Instead, it coincides with his conversion, it is

bound up with the evidence of his changed life, it is one of the results of his salvation, and that, he knows, is 'the gift of God' (Ephesians 2:8). In a classic passage on this theme, John Calvin, one of the greatest theologians of all time, wrote these words: 'Enlightened by [the Holy Spirit], we no longer believe, either on our own judgement or that of others, that the Scriptures are from God; but, in a way superior to human judgement, feel perfectly assured – as much so as if we beheld the divine image impressed on it – that it came to us, by the instrumentality of men, from the very mouth of God.'[4] If you share that experience, you will surely have good reason to enjoy your Bible!

5.
The trouble with translations

One hundred years ago this chapter would have been almost unthinkable; in one hundred years' time it may hardly be necessary! But today is today, and one of the obvious questions a person invited to enjoy their Bible is liable to ask is 'But which Bible?'

Unbelievable as it may seem, the last hundred years have seen at least an equivalent number of new English versions. The Bible has been translated and paraphrased, simplified and amplified. Apart from the better-known productions, this century alone has brought us The Shorter Bible, The Plainer Bible, The Basic Bible, The Better Version, The Authentic Version, The Children's Version (not to be confused with either The Children's New Testament, The Children's Bible or The Young People's Bible!), The Emphasized Bible and The Christian's Bible — to say nothing of The Liverpool Vernacular Gospels and The Cotton Patch Version (in which the author, a gentleman with a Ph.D in Greek, feels free at one point to help his American readers along by translating 'Corinth' as 'Atlanta' and 'Rome' as 'Washington D.C.')!

This gives some idea of the problem we face today, and in spite of the dogmatic statements of some people, for whom preference seems to have become prejudice, the answer to the problem is far from straightforward. At the end of the day, the choice of a version will be a very personal thing, but I believe that a general outline of the history of the Bible in English, and an idea of some of the basic factors behind a good translation will be a help in making that choice. In this chapter, then, I want to consider not one question, but three.

What is the background?

The Bible's journey from its original languages to English is a saga unparalleled in all literature, as even the sketchiest outline will help us to appreciate. The first translation — from the original Hebrew Old Testament into Greek — was the Septuagint (LXX in 'shorthand'), which dates from about 250 B.C. The Latin word *septuaginta* means seventy, and it is thought that about this number of Jewish translators were involved in this work.

When Antiochus Epiphanes, King of Syria, captured Jerusalem in 170 B.C., he decreed that anyone possessing even a part of the Scriptures should be executed. But the Septuagint outlived the Syrian, and many years later the early Christians incorporated it with the New Testament to form the first complete Bible in Greek, the common language of the Middle East in Roman times. In A.D. 303 the Roman Emperor Diocletian mounted a vicious campaign to eliminate the Christian church, and at one stage was so confident he had succeeded that he erected a monument to mark its extinction, and struck a medal commemorating the destruction of the Scriptures. But the Bible survived that butcher, too, and by the time Diocletian died it had spread to areas far beyond the Roman Empire, and been translated into several other languages, including Latin, Syriac, Egyptian and Coptic.

Even more remarkably, Diocletian was succeeded by Constantine, who within a few years proclaimed Christianity as the official state religion of the Roman Empire, and ordered fifty copies of the Greek Scriptures

for use in the churches in his new capital city of
Constantinople!

The next important translation came in A.D. 404,
when the brilliant scholar Jerome, who lived in Bethlehem
at the time, completed a Latin version of the Bible later
known as The Vulgate (from the Latin word *vulgare*,
meaning 'to make public'). Jerome's version was far from
popular at first, but was later to gain such acceptance
that it became England's Bible for a thousand years, and
at the Roman Catholic Council of Trent in 1546 was
declared to be the only authentic Latin Bible.

Nobody is sure when the words of Scripture first
appeared in the English language. Some sections may
date back as far as the seventh century, while Alfred
the Great, more popularly known in connection with
the most famous burnt cakes in history, is among those
who may have translated parts of the Bible into English
during the course of the 200 years that followed.

It was deep into the fourteenth century, however,
before the first major steps were taken towards the first
complete translation of the Bible into English. The name
most commonly associated with this is John Wycliffe,
though he may personally have done little of the actual
translation work. Sometimes called 'the Morning Star
of the Reformation' (which began just over a hundred
years after his death in 1384) it was his passionate conviction that 'the sacred Scriptures are the property of
the people' and he attracted a number of gifted followers who shared his determination that his fellow-
countrymen should have the Bible in their own language.
The first 'Wycliffe' edition, translated direct from the
Vulgate, appeared about the time of his death, and though
its reading was forbidden by law, its handwritten copies
circulated widely, and about 170 of them still exist today.

The next breakthrough came when Scriptures in English
were *printed* for the first time. The key figure here was

William Tyndale, whose determination to get the Bible into the hands of the common people in their own language is best expressed in what were perhaps the most famous words he ever spoke. When a celebrated clergyman was sent to 'convert' him, Tyndale brought the confrontation to an end by telling him, 'If God spares my life, I will take care that a ploughboy shall know more of the Scriptures than you do.' Hounded out of his native land by the ecclesiastical establishment, he found refuge in Germany, completed the first English translation of the New Testament from the Greek, and had it published at Worms in 1526. Tyndale then began to translate the Old Testament from the Hebrew text, helped by Miles Coverdale, another ecclesiastical exile. Tyndale was eventually strangled and burnt to death in 1536, but not before the first printed version of the whole Bible in English was released under Coverdale's name.

The effect of these first English Bibles in printed form was electrifying, and before long other revisions and translations began to appear. There was the Matthew's Bible (1537), a version of Tyndale's work edited by John Rogers under the pen name of Thomas Matthew; the Great Bible (1539), Coverdale's revised version of the Matthew's Bible, which Henry VIII ordered to be chained to the reading-desk in every parish church in the land; and the Geneva Bible (1560), translated in Switzerland by a group of exiles and dedicated to Elizabeth I. With its Old Testament painstakingly based on the Hebrew text, and the New Testament on the best of Tyndale's versions, the Geneva Bible was the finest translation of its time, and remained in print for eighty years.

But all of these were soon to be eclipsed by the most famous English Bible of all time. At the Hampton Court Conference in 1604, King James I of England agreed to a suggestion that work should go ahead on a new translation. Forty-seven of the finest Hebrew and Greek scholars of the day, divided into three groups, worked for over two years and in 1611 the Bible which later became known as the Authorized Version was published. For 300 years this was to be *the* Bible for the entire English-speaking world, and its impact on succeeding generations has been nothing short of monumental.

Until 1881 the Authorized Version reigned without any sign of a serious rival. Then, after ten years of work, and partly based on manuscripts not available in King James's time, the first section (the New Testament) of the Revised Version was published in England. It was considered such a significant event that two Chicago newspapers printed it in full in their Sunday editions (the Gospels, Acts and Romans being telegraphed from New York to beat the publishing deadline). The Old Testament followed in 1885, but neither the Revised Version, nor its transatlantic twin the American Standard Version, published in 1901, ever won popular appeal. This was mainly because in trying to be so minutely accurate in following the original languages word for word they failed to render the result in naturally fluent English. Nevertheless it was the first real challenge to the Authorized Version's monopoly, and before long other major versions were to follow, part of a torrent of translations which has left the English-speaking world knee-deep in Bibles and many Christians hopelessly confused as to which one they should use. So much for the background, which sets the scene for our second question.

What are the basics?

In spite of the deluge of translations we now have, there is no reason why a Christian should find himself taken up with a thoroughly unsound version. But in looking for the best of all he might still find himself juggling several in his mind while being pummelled with conflicting publicity about their respective merits. Rather than jumping straight into a short list of candidates, let us take a look at some of the basic tests we should apply before coming to a decision. Just as 'the law of the Lord is perfect' (Psalm 19:7), so our tests ought to be aimed at establishing the highest possible criteria. What guidelines should we be looking for?

Firstly, we should look for the best men. Notice the plural! The Bible itself tells us that 'Many advisers make victory sure' (Proverbs 11:14) and nowhere is this more obvious than in translating the Bible. It has been estimated that a thorough translation involves an average of thirty points to be taken into consideration in every verse. With 31,173 verses in the Bible, that means 935,190 decisions — a fact which surely demands the safety of team-work. Incidentally, this points up one of the major flaws in many modern *paraphrases*. The best-known in recent years have been The New Testament in Modern English by J. B. Phillips and The Living Bible by Kenneth Taylor. Both can sometimes be useful in giving a quick, general survey of a passage, but the authors freely admit that they have taken many liberties with the text on the basis of their own personal opinions. The one-man paraphrase has certain very limited uses, but it is a totally inadequate substitute for a genuine translation, especially one which is the combined and carefully cross-checked work of a team of highly competent experts. This is not to suggest that the paraphraser is deliberately setting out to delude, but it does mean that he is merely giving us a rough sketch of the real thing.

Then the translators must be *qualified* for the work. We all know what happens when the blind lead the blind! This means that we will be looking for a team of men with a profound knowledge of the original languages, a deep understanding of both the art and science of translation

and a down-to-earth grasp of current English idiom. They
will also need to be qualified spiritually, which basically
means having an unshakeable conviction that the original
Scriptures were 'God-breathed'. This is crucially important; Jesus made it crystal clear that 'The good man brings
good things out of the good stored up in his heart, and
the evil man brings evil things out of the evil stored up
in his heart' (Luke 6:45). At the end of the day, a man's
pen will be guided by his persuasions. To give just one
example, the Christian will immediately rule out such
versions as The New World Translation, the official publication of the heretical Jehovah's Witnesses, because they
deny the deity of Christ, *the* great fundamental of the
Christian faith.

Secondly, we should look for the best manuscript. As
we saw in an earlier chapter, we do not actually possess
any of the original documents from which the books of
our present-day Bible have been translated, and it is only
of those original documents that we can biblically claim
divine inspiration for every word. This immediately places
a great responsibility on the shoulders of Bible translators
because, in the words of J. B. Lightfoot, they must do
their utmost 'to ascertain the exact expression of the
original by the aid of all the critical resources at our command'. Today's Christian can rejoice that these critical
resources are greater now than at any previous time since
the Bible came into print. The vast amount of research
done in this area, and in particular the great number of
manuscripts discovered during the last one hundred years,
has convinced the overwhelming majority of competent
scholars involved that we can get remarkably close to
the original documents. This does not mean to say that
the thousands of ancient manuscripts now discovered are
identical in every detail, but that, regardless of their age,
they agree in a truly remarkable way. Richard Bentley,
one of the earliest textual scholars, put it like this: 'The

real text of the several writers is competently exact in the
worst manuscript now extant; nor is one article of faith or
moral precept either perverted or lost in them; choose as
awkwardly as you will, choose the worst by design, out
of the whole lump of readings . . . even put them into
the hands of a knave or a fool, and yet with the most
sinistrous and absurd choice, he shall not extinguish the
light of any one chapter, nor so disguise Christianity but
that every feature of it will still be the same.'[1]

There is a dogged minority of people who claim that
the only document on which a translation of the New
Testament can properly be based is the seventeenth-century
Greek version which later became known as the 'Received
Text'. The words come from a phrase used by the Dutch
printers Bonaventure and Abraham Elzivir, who in the
preface to the second edition of their work made the
rather extravagant statement: 'The text that you have is
now received by all . . .' The claim was enthusiastic, but
not entirely accurate. The Elzivirs' publication was largely
based on a 1516 translation by their fellow-countryman,
the great Greek scholar Desiderius Erasmus, but that
translation was not without its flaws. Erasmus had only
a handful of Greek manuscripts to work on, none of them
earlier than the twelfth century and none containing the
entire New Testament. For example, he had no Greek
text for the last six verses of Revelation, so he simply translated back into Greek from the Latin Vulgate – with the
result that several words in his finished work had no Greek
manuscript basis at all.

Within ten years, Erasmus's work had been revised
many times in the light of information provided by fresh
Greek manuscripts that had become available. There was
even one instance in which Erasmus agreed to insert a
phrase in his third edition on the understanding that it
had been found in an allegedly new manuscript, but it is
now generally agreed that the manuscript concerned had
been deliberately contrived.

It is perfectly fair to say that the Elzivirs' work was the standard one in use at the time, but to speak of it as the 'Received Text' in the sense that it was unanimously and properly agreed to be the most reliable text that could possibly have been made available, and then to say that it remains so today, is to claim too much. While it is true that the Received Text contains no material error that makes it heretical or untrustworthy, the fact of the matter is that it is an imperfectly edited document based on about 1% of the manuscript evidence now available to us.

Textual criticism is a vast subject, and one which it is obviously not possible to pursue in a book of this size. My only comment at this point would be this: if we are determined to look for the *best*, then at whatever level we feel capable of examining the issue, let us do so honestly, and consider the evidence carefully and courteously. Those who feel unable to study the subject in depth can take comfort in the fact that in the over-ruling providence of God we have thousands of manu-scripts which have been preserved from significant error in a truly remarkable way. We do not have any of the originals, but beyond all doubt we do have material so astonishingly similar that we can truthfully call it the Word of God. As J. Gresham Machen put it, 'God has provided very wonderfully for the plain man who is not a scholar.'

Thirdly, we should look for the best method. Here again, the detailed discussion may be beyond 'Mr Average'— though the end product is very much his concern. Put at its simplest, the translator's job is to translate every word of the original language as accurately as he possibly can, and at the same time to render it in a style and language that is in common use and will be understood clearly by those who read it. To say this produces problems is putting it mildly! For instance, it is not enough to translate the original language word for word, because this would produce chaos in the new language. For example, the literal translation of Romans 9:1 would be 'Truth I say in Christ not I lie witnessing with me the conscience of me in Spirit Holy.' Now what Paul is saying can eventually be un-ravelled from those words, but nobody I know uses that kind of English! (Incidentally, we might note in passing that the Authorized Version translates this verse: 'I say the truth in Christ, I lie not, my conscience also bearing me witness in the Holy Ghost', while the New International Version has 'I speak the truth in Christ — I am not lying, my conscience confirms it in the Holy Spirit.')

On the other hand, the translator dare not lean so far in the direction of the new reader that he parts company with the original writer. The original Scriptures consisted of God's specific words, not his general ideas; they were verbally inspired, not vaguely implied. This means that the translator is not free to pick and choose which words he will include or leave out. He is called to translate the text, not tamper with it. This is another area in which we have only begun to scratch the surface, but again the Christian able to do so will want to examine it more closely and take it into consideration when making his choice.

To put the answer to our second question in one phrase, our basic tests are aimed at helping us to find the trans-lation which conveys with the greatest accuracy and clarity the meaning of the text which, to the best of our current knowledge, is the closest to the original. That sounds clear enough as a general principle: but it still leaves us with our third question.

Which is the best?

In other words, what happens when we try to apply our general principle to the particular translations we have? Should we try to devise a system of marking, with so many

points for the best qualified translators, the purest manuscript, the best method of translation, the clearest English,
and so on? Of course not! Who would dare to claim that in
this way he could take into account every conceivable
factor involved, and then pronounce an infallible judgement? The only thing we can be quite sure of is that none
of our current translations is perfect. There is none in
which every single word has final, divine authority. That
distinction belonged uniquely to the Scriptures *as originally
given*. However, that does not mean that all we can hope
for is 'the best of a bad bunch'. Nor does it mean that we
cannot take any Bible in our hands today and say with
whole-hearted conviction, 'This is the Word of God.'
Rather, we can rejoice at our embarrassment of riches in
having several translations which we can trust to be so
faithfully rendered that God speaks to us through them
as powerfully as he did when he first committed his perfect
Word to imperfect men.

Now let us look at just five of the best-known translations available to us today. For the sake of convenience,
we shall do so in the order in which they were published.

The Authorized Version

AV or not AV? That is the question! Or so it is for many
people. For others, however, there is *no* question; any
suggestion that a 'modern' translation might take the
place of the AV is heresy of the deepest dye. Now that
kind of attitude — and, as we shall see in a moment, it
really does exist — is not far removed from the chestnut
about the superannuated saint who firmly declared, 'If
the Authorized Version was good enough for the apostle
Paul, it is good enough for me!' (Incidentally, the AV
itself *is* a modern translation, because if we condensed
the period from Christ's birth until now into the space
of one day, it was not published until 7.53 pm!)

In trying to assess the AV fairly, let us begin with

some general comments. The title, for instance, has a certain ring of authority about it, but we have no concrete evidence that it was ever 'authorized' at all, because the civic records of the time were destroyed by fire a few years later. But even if it could be proved that it was 'authorized', either by Privy Council or by Parliament as a whole, would that convey upon it final and permanent authority? Would it help to know that it had the blessing of a king who persecuted the Puritans? The New Testament section of the AV is based on the Received Text, but as we saw earlier, this was never 'received' by any official gathering of the church, seeking and sensing God's approval of what they were doing. It was a reprint of an edited version of a few manuscripts, and although it is *essentially* the Word of God, and in no general sense false or heretical, there is powerful evidence that today's translators have access to a text which is very much better. No less an authority than Sir Frederick Kenyon is on record as saying that many of the inaccuracies in the Received Text 'now can be corrected with absolute certainty from the vastly wider information which is at our disposal today'.

Yet in spite of this, and of other detailed points we shall make later, there are those who make the most extravagant claims for the AV, and defend it against all comers with fanatical determination. Quite recently a very earnest Christian sent me a booklet claiming that 'God only wrote *one* Bible' (that Bible being the AV). All modern translations with New Testaments not based entirely on the Received Text are lumped together as 'perversions' and 'wicked counterfeits', based on 'contaminated, Christ-denying manuscripts', and part of 'an attack of Satan against the Holy Word of God'. The AV, on the other hand, is said to be the only Bible 'that God has inspired and safeguarded', the only one that has been 'faithfully translated', the only one that is 'a completely faithful reproduction of the Word of God' and 'the only authoritative and trustworthy Bible'. This same booklet even claims that the seventeenth-century translators of the AV received divine instructions on the placing of every punctuation mark, so that if a man alters so much as a single *comma*, God will 'take away his part out of the book of life'! If that is the case, it certainly seems to put Moses, David, Paul and the other Bible authors in a difficult position, because they did not put the punctuation marks there in the first place! By the same absurd judgement, C. H. Spurgeon would have forfeited his salvation in 1886 because in preaching on Romans 8:1 he followed the reading in the Revised Version (then just four years old) and did not expound the AV words 'who walk not after the flesh, but after the spirit' because he agreed with the revisers that 'this part of my text is not a true portion of Holy Scripture'.

To be perfectly fair, most champions of the AV would not adopt the ridiculous and uncharitable attitude of the booklet I have mentioned, but many would still maintain that it remains the best translation we have, claiming that its theology and language are better than those of any of its rivals. Are they right? To take its theology first, there are certainly places where it *seems* to be weak or at best confusing. In Titus 2:13, for instance, we read that Christians should be 'looking for that blessed hope, and the glorious appearing of the great God *and* our Saviour Jesus Christ'. Could that not be taken to imply that Jesus is not God? 'Our great God and Saviour Jesus Christ' would surely be better, and remove all possible question as to what the phrase means. In 1 Corinthians 11:29 there is the statement that the Christian who receives the sacramental bread and wine unworthily 'eateth and drinketh *damnation* to himself'. Does that not suggest that a Christian can lose his salvation? In Romans 8:16 we are told that 'The Spirit *itself* beareth witness' and in Romans 8:26 that 'The Spirit *itself* maketh intercession.'

In 1 Peter 1:11 it is said of the Spirit of Christ that '*it*
testified'. Do these words not suggest that the Holy Spirit
is a thing and not a Person? In Acts 19:2 Paul is reported
as asking certain people at Ephesus, 'Have ye received the
Holy Ghost *since* ye believed?' Does that not suggest that
a person can be a Christian without receiving the Holy
Spirit? Other examples could be given, and while I am
not for a moment suggesting that the translators of the
AV were theologically corrupt, what I am saying is that
their rendering into English was not always theologically
correct. They were not *deliberately* wrong, but they were
apparently wrong, and to the reader it is what appears that
counts.

On the question of language, there are two sides to the
coin. On the one hand the AV has a dignity, even majesty
of language that no other English version has ever equalled.
It is *superb*, especially in the way in which it often puts
the most profound theological truth into prose that is both
simple and sublime. Its style has shaped the literary culture
of one generation after another, and its influence is still
with us today. But the fact must be faced that the English
it contains is the English of the seventeenth century,
whereas we live in the twentieth century. It has been calculated that about 300 of the words used in the AV had
different meanings then than they do now. For example,
'prevent' (1 Thessalonians 4:15) meant 'precede'; 'conversation' (Philippians 1:27) meant 'behaviour'; 'let' (Romans
1:13) meant 'prevented'. This kind of problem will show
up more vividly if we put another example into a modern
setting. When Paul told the Corinthians, 'Ye are straitened
in your own bowels' (2 Corinthians 6:12) he was complain-
ing at their lack of affection; if you were to tell a person
that today, he might think that you were referring to
some kind of intestinal disorder! And what does the man
in the street make of phrases like 'Moreover, brethren, we
do you to wit of the grace of God' (2 Corinthians 8:1) or

'Jacob sod pottage' (Genesis 25:29)? Then there are all
those word endings familiar 300 years ago, but no longer
in use today. This is surely particularly important when we
realize that the heart of the Bible's message is the gospel,
and that it is meant for every man, and not just for
Christians. Surely we should look for a translation most
likely to be understood clearly by the average person we
meet day by day? If my wife said to a shop assistant, 'My
husband doth desire a hearty meal; wouldst thou be so
kind as to fetch hither a goodly portion of fish fingers?'
he would probably get the message, but he would certainly
think it a little odd, to say the least! Can we really say
that that kind of language is the *best* way to share the
gospel with the world? Might it not give the impression
that our ideas, our religion, our Bible, our gospel *and our
God* are out of date and therefore irrelevant? When 'the
Word became flesh and lived for a while among us' (John
1:14) he spoke the language of the day and of his own
people. Should we not follow his example? The
seventeenth-century preacher William Gurnall said, 'By
being translated, the sword is drawn out of the scabbard.'
But has seventeenth-century English now become a scabbard of its own?

Having said all that we have, we must admit that there
are very substantial points that can be made in favour of
the AV: its translators had a biblical view of the inerrancy
of the original Scriptures; discoveries such as the Dead
Sea Scrolls have underlined the basic reliability of the
Hebrew text from which the Old Testament is translated;
and in spite of its 'olde-worlde' phrases, its rendering of
the original languages into English remains more accurate
than that of many of the more recent translations.

These are some of the issues to be considered with
regard to the AV. Having done so, you will have to decide
whether you believe it remains the best version we have.
Personally, I treasure it deeply, but with the greatest

respect for the opinions of those who differ, I do not believe that it occupies first place by divine right. I think it is priceless; I do not think it is permanent.

The Revised Standard Version

As we noticed earlier in this chapter, the Revised Version (1881) and its American counterpart, the American Standard Version (1901) never achieved wide popularity, mainly because in the attempt to give a literal word-for-word translation their English was stilted and 'wooden'. The copyright of the ASV was later acquired by the International Council of Religious Education, and in 1937 the council authorized its American Standard Bible Committee to undertake a new revision. A total of thirty-two scholars and fifty advisers worked on the task, and eventually the New Testament was published in 1946 and the whole Bible in 1952.

The RSV is therefore a revision of a revision of the AV. In the preface we are told, 'The Revised Standard Version is not a new translation in the language of today. It is not a paraphrase which aims at striking idioms. It is a revision which seeks to preserve all that is best in the English Bible as it has been known and used through the years . . . We have sought to put the message of the Bible in simple, enduring words that are worthy to stand in the great Tyndale-King James tradition. We are glad to say, with the King James translators: "Truly (good Christian Reader) we never thought from the beginning that we should need to make a new translation, nor yet to make of a bad one a good one . . . but to make a good one better."'

Fine words, and many Christians clearly think that the translators have succeeded, because they use the RSV as their basic version. Many churches have opted for it officially, some providing pew copies for those who attend services. While some officially sponsored translations have proved to be 'nine-day wonders', the RSV has steadily held its ground, and has stood up well to the barrage of publicity which has sometimes announced a newer version. What is more, quite a number of commentaries and other study aids are based on the RSV. Perhaps this level of popularity is not too difficult to understand, because if we ignore the RV, for the reasons already given, the RSV was the first real breakthrough (or break-out!) from the AV for the twentieth-century Christian. It is sometimes more accurate in its rendering, and its more modern English is obviously easier to follow. Archaic words have been more or less eliminated, with 'thee', 'thou' and 'thy' being replaced by 'you' and 'your', except where God is being addressed.

But all of this does not necessarily mean that the RSV has won the battle of the Bibles. Many conservative Christians have serious reservations about it and it is taboo in a great number of evangelical churches in America's 'Bible Belt', partly because of its ecumenical sponsorship. But what are the areas of specific criticism? To begin with, expert analysis claims to show some disturbing weaknesses in its technical handling of the text, that is to say, in its grammar and choice of words. A more serious criticism is the translators' handling of the Old Testament. It is generally agreed that the finest basis for any Old Testament translation is the Massoretic Text, named after the Massoretes, Jewish scholars who were active between the sixth and tenth centuries A.D. The Massoretes (the word literally means 'transmitters') were almost un- believably meticulous in the care they took in preserving for succeeding generations a precisely accurate copy of the text they had received. The translators of the AV and the RV held closely to the Massoretic Text, but the RSV departs from it over seventy times in the Psalms alone, and the Old Testament as a whole has a large number of 'corrections', 'revisions' and, more seriously, 'probable reconstructions'. In many cases these represent no more than a translator's best guess as to what might have been the original phrase concerned.

This kind of treatment obviously reflects a more liberal approach than we find in the AV and this same approach colours the RSV translation of certain passages dealing with vitally important doctrines. One of these is the *deity of Christ*. To take just one example, the AV of Romans 9:5, speaking of the Israelites, reads, 'Whose are the fathers, and of whom as concerning the flesh Christ came, who is over all, God blessed for ever. Amen' — a phrase which clearly reflects the truth that Christ is God. But the RSV renders the verse: 'To them belong the patriarchs, and of their race, according to the flesh, is the Christ. God who is over all be blessed for ever.' The difference is both obvious and serious. Nobody is suggesting that the RSV obliterates or obscures the deity of Christ wherever it occurs in the Scriptures, but as weighty a commentator as Charles Hodge says of the traditionally accepted meaning of this particular verse that 'No other interpretation is at all consistent with the grammatical construction, or the relative position of the words,' and that 'There is no reason for . . . torturing the text to make it speak a different language from that commonly ascribed to it.'

Another area in which the RSV is particularly weak is in at least one aspect of the vital doctrine of *atonement*. The argument is too complex to go into in any detail here but, in a nutshell, where the AV uses the word 'propitiation', in places such as Romans 3:25, 1 John 2:2 and 1 John 4:10, the RSV uses the word 'expiation'. Although neither word is in common use today, they are importantly different in meaning. To put it as simply as possible, 'to propitiate' means to appease a person's wrath by means of a sacrifice, whereas 'to expiate' takes no account of the element of God's wrath. When the AV uses the word 'propitiation' it is not only using an accurate translation of the original Greek word but being completely faithful to the Bible's consistent teaching (stated nearly 600 times in the Old Testament alone) that God has a settled,

personal hatred of sin in every form, that man's sin
ruptured his relationship with a holy God, and that something needed to be done to repair that broken relationship.
'Expiation', on the other hand, leaves out the whole idea
of God's anger as a personal quality. One of the RSV's
translators admits this quite freely, and says, 'Any attempt
to show that there was something in the essential nature
of God that demanded satisfaction for sin ends only in
blackening the character of God.' But that line of thinking
is serious error. The Bible does not only teach that on
man's side his sin must be removed, but that on God's
side his wrath must be removed, and that the first can
only be done when the second has taken place. Expiation
only involves getting rid of a problem; propitiation involves
getting right with a person. These are some of the issues
involved in considering the RSV; the thoughtful Christian
will want to weigh them up very carefully before making
his decision.

The New American Standard Bible

Like the RSV, this translation stems from the American
Standard Version, which it describes in its preface as having
been 'a monumental product of applied scholarship,
assiduous labour and thorough procedure'. It was 'a disturbing awareness that the American Standard Version of 1901
was fast disappearing from the scene' that led the Lockman
Foundation to produce this new revision. Its foreword
says that it was produced 'with the conviction that the
words of Scripture as originally penned in the Hebrew and
Greek were inspired by God', and that the purpose of the
NASB was 'to adhere to the original languages of the Holy
Scriptures as closely as possible and at the same time to
obtain a fluent and readable style according to current
English usage'. The work of thirty-two scholars began
with the Gospel of John in 1960 and the entire Bible
appeared in 1971 'with the strong confidence that those

who seek a knowledge of the Scriptures will find herein a source of genuine satisfaction for a clear and accurate rendering of divinely-revealed truth'.

As with the RSV, 'thee', 'thou' and 'thy' have been changed to 'you' and 'your' except when God is being addressed, presumably with the intention of conveying a sense of reverence. In addition, the NASB puts all divine personal pronouns in capital letters, but this commendable aim results in a clumsy appearance. For example, John 14:23 reads, 'Jesus answered and said to him, "If anyone loves Me, he will keep My word; and My Father will love him, and We will come to him, and make Our abode with him."'

An excellent point in the best editions is the inclusion of a great deal of additional information by way of marginal notes. These include cross-references, literal meanings of original words, alternative manuscript readings, explanations of names and places, and notes about weights, measures and money values. Taken together, these constitute a big 'plus' for this particular version.

Its claims for theological soundness are generally borne out very well. In our 'test case' in Romans 9:5, for instance, it has 'Whose are the fathers, and from whom is the Christ according to the flesh, who is over all, God blessed forever. Amen' — which is fine. Nor does it take any chances in the 'propitiation' verses, using exactly that word in all three places. Perhaps its greatest weakness is its failure to convey its very fine translation into *natural*, everyday language. To pick one verse at random, Romans 8:23 reads, 'And not only this, but also we ourselves, having the first-fruits of the Spirit, even we ourselves groan within ourselves, waiting eagerly for our adoption as sons, the redemption of our body.' That is all rather clumsy, and this is unfortunately quite common in this particular version. Nevertheless, it seems to me that the NASB is a worthy candidate in our search for the most helpful translation available to us today.

The Good News Bible

In 1962 the American Bible Society commissioned the eminent Greek scholar Dr Robert Bratcher to begin work on translating the New Testament into 'popular English'. Two years later it approved Dr Bratcher's version of Mark's Gospel, which he called *The Right Time*, and asked him to press ahead with the remainder of the New Testament. With a team of other scholars, he prepared the first draft in just over a year, and 1966 saw the birth of Good News for Modern Man: The New Testament in Today's English Version. The translation of the Old Testament took another ten years, and it was not until 1976 that the complete Bible was available and published under the shorter title Good News Bible.

The most obvious feature of the GNB is the inclusion of about 500 line drawings to illustrate the text. These are remarkably simple and at times quite striking, though many sensitive Christians object to Christ being represented as a kind of 'matchstick man'. As well as the usual chapters and verses, the text is helpfully divided into subject sections, with clear and simple headings. Another major feature is the section of helps added at the end of the Bible. This has a word list, an index (mainly the names of people and places, but including some subjects), a list of Septuagint readings (New Testament passages quoted or paraphrased from the Septuagint) and an outline chart of Bible history. Within the Bible itself, each of the sixty-six books has a brief introduction, and there are several geographical maps.

These features obviously back up GNB's major aim, which is to get the Bible's message across in a direct and helpful way. As far as the translation is concerned, this means using simpler words and shorter sentences. There is a striking example of the latter in Ephesians 1:3–14, where one sentence in the AV becomes fourteen in GNB.

How does GNB deal with our 'test case'? Although a

footnote does allow two alternatives, the actual text reads, 'They are descended from the famous Hebrew ancestors; and Christ, as a human being, belongs to their race. May God, who rules over all, be praised for ever! Amen.' One would have preferred it put differently. The same vital doctrine suffers even greater violence in Philippians 2:6, where we are told that Jesus 'did not think that by force he should try to become equal with God' — a phrase which surely suggests that he was not eternally divine. This particular verse is notoriously difficult to translate, but the GNB version is frankly appalling.

What of the 'propitiation' verses? The GNB has 'the means by which our sins are forgiven', which is the truth, but not the whole truth, because it misses the point about the personal wrath of God and the need for appeasement. To mention just one other doctrinal passage: one notices that in the famous prophecy in Isaiah 7:14 the AV word 'virgin' is translated 'young woman', with a footnote that many evangelical scholars well qualified to debate the point will find unsatisfactory.

To sum up, the GNB is lively and readable, and will probably make some impact for a time. The question is whether in its attempt to be sufficiently popular it has failed to be sufficiently precise. At the end of the day, I think that the publishers' suggestion that this could prove to be 'the most significant publishing event in the English-speaking world since the Authorized Version was released in 1611' will prove more enthusiastic than accurate!

The New International Version

This is the last of the translations we shall look at here, and is the most recent of those we are examining. After ten years of preliminary study, an interdenominational group of biblical scholars agreed in 1965, at a meeting held in Palos Heights, Illinois, that a new translation of the Bible was needed. Their decision met with widespread support and was endorsed by a representative body of church leaders at a meeting in Chicago in 1966. In 1967 the project was officially sponsored by the New York Bible Society International, which until then had not backed any other translation except the AV. The New Testament section of the New International Version was published in 1973 and the entire Bible in 1978.

There are several general things that immediately commend the NIV. In the first place, I am impressed by its *translators.* Over one hundred distinguished international scholars were involved in the translation and the preface tells us that they were all 'united in their commitment to the authority and infallibility of the Bible as God's Word in written form'. In other words, its basis is thoroughly evangelical, which means that we can be sure that any textual weaknesses it may have are not the result of deliberate attempts to dilute or distort essential biblical truth.

Then I am impressed with the great *care* taken over the work. The system of reviewing and revising was extraordinarily detailed and included testing the translation for clarity and ease of reading among a wide age range of people from many walks of life. In this area I am also impressed by the *humility* shown in its production. In the early stages, editions of individual books of the Bible were described as preliminary translations and welcomed suggestions and criticisms, a number of which were eventually incorporated into the first printing of the entire Bible.

These may be some of the reasons why there is growing support for the NIV in many English-speaking parts of the world. In Britain, for instance, the Gideons International, which had previously used nothing but the AV in its free distribution of the Scriptures in schools, agreed that local branches could use the NIV New Testament if they preferred. Within a year the vast majority had switched to using the NIV, under the title of The Modern English Version. In British churches, too, there would seem to be evidence that among those changing to twentieth-century versions the NIV is becoming the majority choice.

The NIV is not based on the Received Text, nor on any other single text, but on those carefully judged to be the best Hebrew, Aramaic or Greek sources available at each point. As with the GNB, it has changed the archaisms into modern English and divided the body of the text into clearly defined sections. The style used is modern and clear without being racy. Although it is not a word for word translation like the NASB, it does attempt to acknowledge each original word in some way and has succeeded in combining a high degree of accuracy with a fluent, readable style. It takes fewer liberties than the GNB and does not chop up the long AV sentences into such small pieces. The passage in Ephesians which is one sentence in the AV and fourteen in the GNB is seven in the NIV.

Doctrinally, the NIV is generally excellent. Our 'test case' in Romans 9:5 reads, 'Theirs are the patriarchs, and from them is traced the human ancestry of Christ, who is God over all, for ever praised! Amen' – which clearly reflects the deity of Christ. There are places where the full glory of Christ's deity comes across even more clearly than in the AV. In Colossians 1:19 for instance, the AV says of Christ, 'It pleased the Father that in him should all fulness dwell'; the NIV has 'For God was pleased to have all *his* fulness dwell in him.' In Philippians 2:9 the AV says, 'Wherefore God also hath highly exalted him, and given him a name which is above every name'; the NIV has 'Therefore God exalted him to the highest place and gave him *the* name that is above every name.' In some ways, the NIV is closer to the Greek than most former translations. An excellent example of this is at

2 Timothy 3:16, where 'all Scripture is God-breathed' is much more helpful than 'given by inspiration of God' (AV) or 'inspired by God' (NASB and GNB).

In the 'propitiation' passages, the NIV has 'sacrifice of atonement' (Romans 3:25) and 'atoning sacrifice for our sins' (1 John 2:2; 1 John 4:10). This is a little disappointing, but it does retain the important objective reference missing in the RSV's 'expiation'. In fairness to all modern translations, one ought to say that there seems no concise, common and clear way to convey the exact and full meaning of the Greek word *hilasterion* in the English language. However, the NIV does help by putting a superb footnote to each of the three 'propitiation' verses, explaining that in acting as a propitiation Christ turned away God's wrath and took away our sins. This makes it crystal clear that the NIV is in no way seeking to weaken the meaning of the verses concerned.

There is no doubt in my mind that the NIV has a very strong claim to be the finest version now available in the English language. Like all other translations (including the AV) it has weaknesses and inconsistencies, but they have no sinister intent and one can always make marginal notes to point these out as they become known. I became a 'convert' to the NIV soon after it began to be published and I can certainly testify that it has had a marked effect on my reading and study of Scripture and on all my preaching and writing ministry. Will it prove to be the best? That remains to be seen, and at the end of the day the choice of a Bible version is an issue on which everyone should seek to be 'fully convinced in his own mind' (Romans 14:5).

If there could be a broad consensus in favour of one sound version it would avoid a great deal of the confusion caused by the current deluge of translations. Let me offer you two pieces of advice as you seek to come to your own conclusion on the issue. Firstly, *compare several versions.*

Study them side by side. Weigh them up against each other.
Ask for advice from mature Christians, especially those
who have studied the issues involved. Look out for reviews,
listen for comments, and then see for yourself whether
you agree with them, and what importance you give to
them. Secondly, and as soon as possible, *concentrate on
one version*, and do most of your reading from the same
edition. Chopping and changing versions will cause no
end of problems; deciding on one, and then reading constantly from the same copy, will help the memory to
'place' passages of Scripture more easily, and in that way
help you to enjoy your Bible.

6.
A look around the library

The members of my family are very keen readers, with
the result that visits to the library are not only frequent
but major operations. To increase the number of books
available to us, we eventually joined a second library,
a large five-storey complex with a vast number of books
apparently covering every subject under the sun. Yet
these thousands of volumes are not just lying about in
unclassified heaps. They are carefully arranged, catalogued
and indexed, so that borrowers can quickly find the
particular book they need. We are familiar with the layout
now, but on our first visit we spent quite a long time
taking a look around, getting the general lie of the land.

This is the kind of point we have reached in this book.
Following on from what we have learned so far, we are
now ready to make a general survey of the Bible as a
whole — in other words, to take a look around the library.
To help us to get a good all-round picture, let us look at
it from three different angles.

The recognition of the canon

The Greek word *kanon* originally meant a reed used as a
measuring instrument, and later a fixed standard or norm.
Eventually it was used to define the writings acknowledged
to have divine inspiration and final authority, that is to say,

the collection of sixty-six books we have in the Bible. But why these sixty-six? Who decided which books should be included in the library? And when was the decision taken?

We can begin to answer those questions from the Bible itself. In an earlier chapter we noticed that in the Old Testament alone we read phrases like 'God said' and 'the word of the Lord came' about 4,000 times, and it is obvious that the words that follow must have divine authority, in other words, *canonicity*. But it is fascinating to trace the way in which the sixty-six pieces of the canonical jigsaw fitted into place over the years.

For the sake of simplicity we can say that the first part of the canon consisted of the Pentateuch, the first five books of the Bible. These were written by Moses, who made it crystal clear that when he claimed to speak and write God's words, he meant precisely that. To give just one example, he writes that God commanded him to say to the people of Israel, 'You have seen for yourselves that *I have spoken to you from heaven*' (Exodus 20:22). His writings bore the same stamp of authority until just before his death, when we read that Moses 'finished writing in a book the words of this law' and that he solemnly ordered the priests to 'take this book of the law and place it beside the ark of the covenant of the Lord your God' (Deuteronomy 31:24–26). To those ancient Jews, nothing could have given those writings a more impressive seal of approval.

We can see this confirmed later on in the Old Testament. If we jump 300 years we find King David on his deathbed, telling his son Solomon to 'observe what the Lord your God requires: Walk in his ways, and keep his decrees and commands, his laws and requirements, as written in the Law of Moses' (1 Kings 2:3). Another 300 years later, we read of King Amaziah seeking to govern the people 'in accordance with what is written in the Book of the Law

of Moses *where the Lord commanded . . .*' (2 Kings 14:6).
Yet another 400 years, and we discover the Jews swearing
a solemn oath 'to follow the Law of God *given through
Moses*' (Nehemiah 10:29). Throughout these centuries
the 'law of Moses' was clearly regarded as the law of God.
The part of the Bible that has been attacked the loudest
has been approved the longest!

When we come to the writers who followed Moses, we
see the same kind of *written* authority. For example, we
are told that Joshua in confirming the words of Moses,
'recorded these things in the Book of the Law of God'
(Joshua 24:26) and that Samuel 'explained to the people
the regulations of the kingship. He *wrote* them down on a
scroll and deposited it before the Lord' (1 Samuel 10:25).
Then we have a fascinating glimpse of the prophet Jeremiah
at work with his private secretary, a man called Baruch:
'And while Jeremiah dictated all the words the Lord had
spoken to him, Baruch wrote them on the scroll' (Jeremiah
36:4). Many years later, Daniel had no hesitation in gauging
the timing of certain events by reading 'the word of the
Lord given to Jeremiah the prophet' (Daniel 9:2).

We cannot take time to look at other examples, but the
picture is clear: God spoke to chosen men, those men
wrote down what God said and God's people recognized
the divine authority of their words. In this way the canon
of Scripture slowly expanded. Nobody can be quite sure
when the books which later came to be known as the Old
Testament were first collected together, but this was
probably done by about 200 B.C. Although they contained
all the material we now have in our Old Testament, there
were certain differences in arrangement. There were only
twenty-two books, for instance, instead of our thirty-nine.
This was due to a different method of grouping; for
example, the twelve books from Hosea to Malachi were
counted as one. Then the twenty-two books were divided
into three main sections, known as The Law, The Prophets

and The Writings. Finally, the sections were placed in order, the complete collection beginning, as ours does, with Genesis, but ending with Chronicles.

These differences are not important, of course, but what it is vital to notice is that *this 'Hebrew Bible' was the one Jesus used and confirmed.* Accusing his religious enemies of following in the footsteps of those who in previous generations had hounded God's faithful servants to death, he spoke of 'the blood of all the prophets that has been shed since the beginning of the world, from the blood of Abel to the blood of Zechariah, who was killed between the altar and the sanctuary' (Luke 11:50). Abel's death is the first martyrdom recorded in Genesis and Zechariah's the last recorded in Chronicles. By linking them together, Jesus was not only including all the Old Testament martyrs (literally from A to Z!) he was also locating and limiting the Old Testament canon, and saying that it ran from Genesis to Chronicles or, as we would say today, from Genesis to Malachi.

But on at least two other occasions, Jesus gave even clearer confirmation of the Old Testament canon. Shortly after his resurrection he spoke to two disciples on the road to Emmaus, and 'beginning with Moses and all the Prophets, he explained to them what was said *in all the Scriptures* concerning himself' (Luke 24:27). Later, when he met with a larger group of Christians, he told them, 'Everything must be fulfilled that is written about me in the Law of Moses, the Prophets and the Psalms' (Luke 24:44) – covering all three parts of the Hebrew Bible. Taken together, these statements of Jesus give nothing less than divine underlining to the fact that the Jewish people held in their hands the authoritative Word of God. It is also interesting to notice that although he often rebuked the religious leaders of his day for misinterpreting the Scriptures, or twisting them to meet their own ends, *he never once accused them of adding to them or subtracting from them.* That surely suggests that he believed that only God's Word, and all of God's Word, had been faithfully and accurately preserved over the centuries. In this connection, it is fascinating to compare the words of the famous Jewish historian Josephus who in about A.D. 100 wrote, 'For we have not an innumerable multitude of books among us, disagreeing from, and contradicting one another, but only twenty-two books which contain the records of all the past times, which are justly believed to be divine.' He then went on to say that 'During so many ages . . . no one has been so bold as either to add anything to them, to take anything from them, or to make any change in them; but it is become natural to all Jews . . . to esteem these books to contain divine doctrines, and to persist in them, and if occasion be, willingly to die for them.' This is a very impressive addition to the reasons why we can confidently accept the divine authority of the Old Testament we have today.

As far as the canon of the New Testament is concerned, we have covered some of the most important ground already. This was in chapter 3, when we looked at the internal evidence for the divine authority of the writers — the plain, straightforward statements that, like the Old Testament prophets, these men were writing on God's instructions. This is the same as saying that their writings were part of the canon *as soon as they were written.* As each book came into being, so it became part of Scripture. We can see this very clearly by noticing Peter's statement about Paul's writings, which, he said, 'ignorant and unstable people distort, as they do *the other Scriptures*' (2 Peter 3:16). Even at that early stage, a devout Jew like Peter accepted Paul's writings as being on a par with the sacred Old Testament Scriptures; to him, they were part of the Word of God.

The very word 'distort' actually leads us to the next step in tracing how our Bible was completed. During the first century, the writings of the apostles and their close associates were circulated and exchanged among the new churches that were being founded. We get a glimpse of this in one of Paul's epistles, where he writes, 'After this letter has been read to you, see that it is also read in the church of the Laodiceans and that you in turn read the letter from Laodicea' (Colossians 4:16). But after a while, two problems arose. One was the gradual death of the apostles, and the other was the fact that false documents began to circulate. One of the chief culprits was Marcion, a wealthy businessman who about the year A.D. 150 began to establish his own churches and circulate his own 'canon'. As with so much heresy, Marcion's particular brand was a mixture of fact and fiction. He included Luke's Gospel and ten of Paul's epistles, for instance, though he doctored them to fit in with his own unbiblical ideas. Faced with this kind of situation, the Christian church needed to know for certain which books had the seal of divine authority.

It is impossible to unravel the whole story of how this was done, but we can trace parts of it. One of the most tantalizing glimpses comes as early as about A.D. 130, when Polycarp, the Bishop of Smyrna, wrote to Christians at Philippi and quoted from the Gospels as being part of Scripture. About fifty years later the great scholar Irenaeus quoted freely from both the Gospels and the epistles, and again treated them as Scripture.

By A.D. 200 some twenty of our New Testament books had been accepted by virtually the entire Christian church. This situation was confirmed about a century later by Eusebius of Caesarea (who died about A.D. 340 and has been called 'the father of church history'). He drew up a document confirming that the entire church accepted twenty books, and that only a minority had doubts about the remaining seven — Hebrews, James, 2 Peter, 2 and 3 John, Jude and Revelation. By the time the Council of

Laodicea was held in 363, only Revelation was in doubt, and at the Synod of Hippo, held in 393, it too was included in the list. Finally, the Council of Carthage in 397 became the first universal gathering of Christians to confirm the church's acceptance of the twenty-seven New Testament books we now have, decreeing that 'Besides the canonical Scriptures nothing be read in the church under the title of the divine Scriptures.' From that day to this, not a single book has been added to or taken away from the list of sixty-six books in the canon of Scripture as we have it (though at the Council of Trent in 1546, the Roman Catholic Church extended its official endorsement to the Apocrypha, a strange collection of inferior writings which were not a part of the original Hebrew Scriptures).

That is a very brief outline of how the books in the Bible came together — but what a fascinating story it is! No library in the world has ever been so carefully chosen. Accepting the Old Testament for the reasons we have already seen, generations of godly men spent about 350 years sifting and analysing the collection of first-century writings before they made their historic declaration. During the whole of that time, very stringent tests were applied. For a book to be recognized as canonical it had to be written by one of the apostles or their close associates; it had to show that it had been accepted and used by Christians at large from the time when it was written; and its doctrine had to fit perfectly into every other interlocking part of the Scriptures being built up. Yet that does not mean that the final choice was no more than 'a committee decision'. As somebody has rightly said, 'The Bible is not an authorized collection of books, but a collection of authorized books.' The church has never had the power to *authenticate* Scripture; all it has ever had is the duty *to acknowledge* it — and the ability to exercise that duty could only be given by the Holy Spirit.

In Paul's words, 'We have not received the spirit of the world but the Spirit who is from God, that we may understand what God has freely given us' (1 Corinthians 2:12). That truth has been tested for nearly two thousand years, and it still stands. Today's Christian knows that every book in the divine library is fact and not fiction, because the Author tells him so! So much for the recognition of the canon. Now let us look at the Bible from another angle.

The relationship of the covenants

At the beginning of this chapter we noted that in a public lending library all the books are carefully classified, usually according to subject matter, while in each section the books are arranged in a specific way, such as in alphabetical order of the author's surnames. Are the Bible's contents arranged in that kind of order? Yes and no! We have already seen that the books were rearranged several times. Nor are they in strictly *chronological* order. In the Old Testament, for example, Hosea appears four books later than Jeremiah in our present Bible, although it actually dates from about 150 years earlier. In the New Testament, the Epistle of James was possibly the very first book to be written, but it has been 'filed' almost at the end of the collection. Nor, for that matter, are the books in *doctrinal* order. You cannot follow the whole body of Christian doctrine straight through from one book to the next; instead the same truths are scattered throughout the whole Bible, and emphasized more in some places than in others. This all adds up to saying that the books of the Bible are not in *infallible* order. Their classification is not part of their inspiration. The Bible we hold in our hands today is certainly God's Word, but it was not written in this order, any more than it was written in this language.

But having said all of that, the men who gathered these

sixty-six books together would obviously have done so with care and prayer, and it should therefore be no surprise to us to find that there is a distinct and logical order in the Bible after all. What in fact the 'librarians' did was to assemble the books into sections, basing their classification very generally on the nature of the books concerned.

To anybody coming to the Bible for the first time, the one major division would seem to be that into the Old and New Testaments. Yet that word 'division' can be deceptive. There is certainly a division in *time*, with a gap of about 400 years between Malachi and Matthew. But there is no division of *theme*. Both Old and New Testaments tell us of the eternal God's sovereign creation of the universe, of man's deliberate fall into sin, of God's provision of salvation and of man's responsibility to exercise repentance, faith and obedience. Instead of thinking of the Bible as being *divided* into the Old and New Testaments, it would be better if we thought of these two sections as being *united* into one Bible. This unity is seen to perfection when we link two statements made by Jesus. On one occasion he said of the Old Testament writings, 'These are the Scriptures that *testify about me*' (John 5:39), while later he promised the disciples that when the Holy Spirit came 'he will *testify about me*' (John 15:26). The Lord Jesus Christ gives unity and authority to the whole Bible from Genesis to Revelation.

We can see the same truth by realizing that the word 'testament' is the same as 'covenant', and that it was by means of a covenant (a sovereign declaration of intent) that God had promised to bless his people. If we bear this in mind, the relationship between the 'old' and 'new' covenants becomes clear when we read that, in the birth of Jesus, God came 'to show mercy to our fathers and to remember his holy covenant, the oath he swore to our father Abraham' (Luke 1:72, 73). The same truth comes vividly across when Jesus speaks of his death as 'my blood

of the covenant, which is poured out for many for the
forgiveness of sins' (Matthew 26:28). These statements
make it crystal clear that we have one God, not two; one
Saviour, not two; one revelation, not two. Recognizing
this will help us to avoid the false notion that God's revelation in the Old Testament is in some way inferior to that in
the New Testament. Nothing could be further from the
truth. The attributes and character of God, the nature of
man, and the realities of the believer's experience are
perfectly expressed in the Old Testament and are repeated
and underlined throughout the New Testament.

We can put this yet another way by saying that although
the Old and New Testaments are different from each
other, they are dependent on each other. One theologian
has said that the Old and New Testaments are like the
two halves of a sentence; both are necessary before we
can read the whole sentence. The Puritan preacher Thomas
Watson put it even better when he said, 'The two Testaments are the two lips by which God has spoken to us.'

Nevertheless there are certain differences between the
Old and New Testaments, and one way to summarize them
would be to take up that comment about the two halves
of a sentence and say that in the New Testament God
completed saying what he began to say in the Old. He
revealed part of the plan of salvation to Adam, another
part to Noah, more to Abraham, even more to David,
and so on, until in the person of Jesus Christ its full
glory was revealed. As the writer to the Hebrews put it,
'In the past God spoke to our forefathers through the
prophets at many times and in various ways, but in these
last days he has spoken unto us by his Son' (Hebrews
1:1, 2). The Old Testament was the truth, but not the
whole truth! In its pages God spoke slowly, gradually,
progressively. But in Jesus Christ he spoke fully, freely
and finally. Jesus was not merely the last of many messen-
gers, but the very message itself. That is why even John

the Baptist, whom the Bible describes as the greatest of all the prophets, admits that he himself was not 'the light' but rather that, like all the other prophets, 'he came only as a witness to the light' (John 1:8).

In one of his books, the well-known theologian Dr W. H. Griffith Thomas imagines someone who only possessed an Old Testament. Having read it through, he would come to the conclusion that here was a book of unfulfilled promises, unexplained ceremonies and unsatisfied longings. But if he was then handed a New Testament, he would discover that on the very first page the birth of Jesus is described as taking place 'to fulfil what the Lord has said through the prophet' (Matthew 1:22). As he read on, he would soon find that in Christ's birth, life, death, resurrection, ascension and promised return all those Old Testament promises are fulfilled, all the ceremonies explained and all the longings satisfied. The Bible, then, is to be seen, read and studied *as a whole*, with every part contributing to every other part. Approach the Bible with this conviction and you will find new light on every page!

A review of the contents

Without withdrawing a word from the previous section, we can only examine the Bible as we find it, and this will obviously mean keeping to the familiar outline of Old and New Testaments.

The arrangement of the Old Testament

For the sake of simplicity, we can say that the thirty-nine books of the Old Testament are arranged into three categories — history, poetry and prophecy. Of these, history and prophecy each account for seventeen titles, and poetry for the remaining five. Another 'memory aid' is the fact that both the history and prophecy sections are divided into two sub-sections of five and twelve. In the history section, the first five books are by Moses, while the others take the story forward from Joshua to Esther. In the prophecy section, the first five books (Isaiah—Daniel) are by far the largest, and their writers are therefore known as the Major Prophets. The writers of the other twelve books (Hosea—Malachi) are called the Minor Prophets, though, of course, their writings are equally important because equally inspired. If we put all of this in the form of a diagram, it would look like this:

History		Poetry	Prophecy	
Moses	Others		Major	Minor
5	12	5	5	12

This can be a very simple way of beginning a system of memorizing the broad outline of the Old Testament. Each of the thirty-nine books comes in one of three sections. If it is not poetry, it is either history (the first section) or prophecy (the last section). Of course you may already be able to rattle off all thirty-nine books by heart, and find any one of them instantly, but some readers of this book may not yet be at that stage, so please be patient with me during this very basic passage!

Perhaps this is the place to insert a brief outline of the *contents* of the Old Testament, again as a simple 'index'. We can do this best by keeping to the three main divisions we have already mentioned.

1. History
Genesis, of course, begins by recording the history of creation and of man's fall into sin. Then comes the earliest

'family tree', from Adam to Noah. The call of Abraham
(Genesis 12) marks the beginning of God's detailed dealings with a chosen people. This is the theme of the
remainder of the book, which includes the lives of
Abraham, Isaac, Jacob (later called Israel), Esau and
Joseph, and ends with the death of Joseph in Egypt.
Exodus tells of the Israelites' miraculous release from
slavery in Egypt and part of their experience in the wilderness. The key figure is Moses, and the most important
events after the escape from Egypt are the giving of the
Ten Commandments and other laws at Mount Sinai and
the building of the tabernacle. Although we have included
it in the history section, *Leviticus* has no 'movement' in
it at all. Its twenty-seven chapters consist entirely of
religious and social laws given by God through Moses
to the Israelites. It is left to *Numbers* to trace the remainder
of their wilderness wanderings from Sinai to the borders
of the promised land of Canaan, a journey of thirty-eight
years. *Deuteronomy* contains the final words of Moses to
the people of Israel. A whole generation had died in the
wilderness, and in this series of addresses Moses reminds
the new generation of their history and of God's binding
laws given at Sinai (Deuteronomy means 'repetition of the
law').

Joshua tells of the Israelites' conquest of Canaan, and
of the ways in which the land was divided among the
tribes. *Judges* records about 170 turbulent years of history
under twelve successive but not always successful 'judges'.
After the lovely story of *Ruth*, one of Christ's ancestors,
1 Samuel takes up the general story. It begins with the
birth of Samuel, the last of the judges. Against his advice,
the people clamoured for a king, and Saul was chosen.
But he fell into disgrace and David was anointed king at
Bethlehem. David's friendship with Jonathan, his running
battle with the demented Saul, and his famous fight with
the Philistine hero Goliath are highlights in a book which

ends with Saul committing suicide. *2 Samuel* records the triumphs and tragedies of King David's life and reign. David's place was taken by his son Solomon, whose reign is covered by the early part of *1 Kings*. But Solomon, God's 'wise man', eventually slid into idolatry and his kingdom split into two. Ten rebel tribes united under Jeroboam to form the northern kingdom of Israel, while the remaining two tribes remained loyal to Solomon's son Rehoboam and became the southern kingdom of Judah. The remainder of 1 Kings and all of *2 Kings* carefully plot the ups and downs of both kingdoms over a period of about 400 years, until both were captured and their people deported. The ten tribes of Israel were taken to Assyria and are never heard of again. The two southern tribes were taken to Babylonia, where they were held captive for over half a century. 1 and 2 Kings also record the activities of the great prophets Elijah and Elisha, and it was during this same period that several of the Bible's prophetical books were written, including Amos and Hosea (prophecies delivered to the northern kingdom of Israel) and Isaiah, Jeremiah, Micah, Nahum, Habakkuk and Zephaniah (prophecies delivered to the southern kingdom of Judah). For the most part, *1 and 2 Chronicles* repeat the history of 2 Samuel and 1 and 2 Kings, but concentrate on events of particular religious importance.

When Cyrus, the founder of the Persian Empire, conquered Babylonia, one of his first acts was to release the Jewish prisoners, allowing those who wished to do so to return to Jerusalem to rebuild the temple. *Ezra* and *Nehemiah* have this report, which is the most 'modern' history in the Old Testament. *Esther* is remarkable in that it never mentions God by name, but it is a wonderful example of his overruling in men's lives.

2. Poetry
Job is a poetic treatment of history — the story of a man

who served truthfully, suffered terribly and survived triumphantly. The *Psalms* may have been written over a period of about 1,000 years and eventually became the Jews' hymn book (authorized version!). They are divided into five sections (1–41; 42–72; 73–89; 90–106 and 107–150) and cover a marvellous variety of religious experiences. *Proverbs* could be called 'God's transistorized wisdom' because of the brilliantly concise way in which it conveys divine truth on a great number of subjects. *Ecclesiastes* contains the reflections of a wise and godly philosopher on the meaning of life. The *Song of Solomon* speaks of the purity of human love and points to a love that is even greater.

3. Prophecy

Of the five 'major' books of the prophets, *Isaiah*, *Jeremiah* and *Lamentations* are from the period prior to the final collapse of the divided kingdom, while *Ezekiel* and *Daniel* both tell us that they are dated during the captivity in Babylonia. Of the 'minor' books, *Hosea*, *Joel*, *Amos*, *Obadiah*, *Jonah*, *Micah*, *Nahum*, *Habakkuk* and *Zephaniah* are before the exile, and the other three, *Haggai*, *Zechariah* and *Malachi*, come from the period after the Jews had returned home. Taken as a whole, these books proclaim God's Word, predict his judgements on the disobedient and promise his blessing to those who repent.

The arrangement of the New Testament

Like their thirty-nine Old Testament counterparts, the twenty-seven books in the New Testament are in sensible but not infallible order; the different *sections* are clear, but the books are not placed in the precise order in which they were written, nor do they contain clear-cut themes that follow on in logical sequence.

Yet, as with the Old Testament, we can divide the New Testament into three sections, and again two of them are history and prophecy. The largest section consists of epistles (or letters) written either to individual Christians or to Christian congregations. Although it lacks any balance, let us also put this New Testament arrangement down in the form of a diagram:

History	Letters	Prophecy
5	21	1

When we come to jot down the *outline* of the New Testament books, we may find that this is best done by passing more quickly over the historical section and concentrating a little more on the letters, as most of the history books cover the same ground.

1. History

The history section is obviously sub-divided into the four Gospels (the biographies of Jesus Christ) and the Acts of the Apostles. Of the Gospels, those by *Matthew, Mark* and *Luke* are sometimes called the Synoptic Gospels, because they contain a great deal of common material (the word 'synoptic' comes from two Greek words meaning 'to view together'). As an illustration of this, only about thirty verses in Mark (which was probably the first to be written) do not have a parallel in Matthew or Luke. Matthew and Luke record the events surrounding the birth of Jesus, then all three books take up the story when Jesus is about thirty years of age. They then tell of his life, teaching, miracles, death, resurrection and ascension. But although they cover the same general ground, they do have particular emphases. Matthew obviously wrote with Jews in mind and concentrated on showing Jesus to be the promised Messiah. Mark was clearly aiming at the Gentiles and made comparatively little reference to the Old Testament. Luke originally wrote to give an accurate account of the life of Jesus to a man called Theophilus. The Gospel of *John*, which probably dates from about A.D. 90, was written to convince people of the deity of Christ. It records no parables, but gives special emphasis to miracles which underlined Christ's claims to be divine.

After the Gospels we come to the *Acts of the Apostles*. Also written by Luke to Theophilus, it covers the thirty explosive first years of the Christian church. The events on the Day of Pentecost, the death of Stephen, the first Christian martyr, the conversion and missionary journeys of the apostle Paul and the evangelistic and other activities of the apostles are all woven together in this exhilarating account.

2. Letters
Of the twenty-one letters, thirteen were written by the apostle Paul, three by John, two by Peter and one each by James and Jude; another (Hebrews) is anonymous. Paul's letters are placed first.

Romans is a theological 'block-buster', the greatest written statement of fundamental Christian doctrine in the world. Its great theme is God's way of salvation, provided in the death of Christ on behalf of sinners, a gift to be received by faith. *1 Corinthians* tackles problems that had arisen within the church, including questions about marriage, immorality, the place of women in the church and the Christian ministry. It also includes a famous chapter on love. *2 Corinthians* is an intensely personal letter in which Paul tells of his love and concern for the church and writes about the nature of true apostleship. *Galatians* was written to Gentile converts in Asia Minor who were in danger of being hoodwinked by false teaching which said that, as well as faith in Christ, obedience to the Old Testament ceremonial law was necessary for salvation. Paul's brilliant argument demolishes this subtle attack on the gospel. *Ephesians* contains the most marvellous statements about the unity, beauty and duty of the Christian church. *Philippians* was written from prison, but is full of triumphant joy rooted in the certainty of eternal union with Christ. *Colossians* shows Christ as the Head of the church, and warns against any high-sounding philosophy that might draw Christians away from this great truth. *1 and 2 Thessalonians* both breathe the air of the apostle's great concern for an infant church, their main theme being the second coming of Christ. *1 and 2 Timothy* and *Titus* are sometimes called the Pastoral Epistles, because they were written to men with pastoral responsibilities in local churches — Timothy in Ephesus and Titus on the island of Crete. Together, the three letters deal with many aspects of local church life. *Philemon* is a covering letter returning a runaway slave to his owner, yet contains important teaching on human relationships and Christian fellowship.

Hebrews, as its title implies, was written to Jewish Christians. It has two main themes, the superiority of Christ over all the priests and prophets of the Old Testament, and even over the angels, and the responsibility of Christians to exercise whole-hearted faith in their Saviour.

James is one of the earliest New Testament books. Its great concern is that a person claiming to be a Christian must demonstrate the reality of his faith by the quality of his life. *1 and 2 Peter* both recognize that Christians, living as they do in a sinful world, will have to face persecution, scorn and heresy; these books tell believers how to cope with them. *1 John* speaks of God as being 'light', 'life' and 'love', and shows the way to confident Christian discipleship. *2 and 3 John* are two brief 'memos'; together, they touch on virtues such as truth, love, obedience and generosity, and the vices of heresy and pride. *Jude* is very similar to parts of 2 Peter and deals with heretical teaching within the church.

3. Prophecy

Revelation is a majestic yet mysterious book. Mainly
through a series of spectacular visions, it assures hard-
pressed believers of the certainty of Christ's return to
the earth and of God's ultimate and universal triumph.

Perhaps even this quick dash through the Bible will
have whetted your appetite to read it *all* and to read it
as a whole. Of course, this has been no more than an
'index' to what you will find, but there are several excellent books which give a much fuller picture. Of these,
The Lion Handbook to the Bible (Lion Publishing) is a
superb full-colour production which it is exhilarating to
use. Its sixty articles, over 400 pictures and nearly 100
maps and charts will not only give you an excellent overall guide to the Bible, it will help to make it 'live'! At a
deeper level, William Hendriksen's *Survey of the Bible*
(Evangelical Press) will be a great help, especially with
its careful analysis of each of the sixty-six books. These
two volumes would be an excellent investment for anyone who wants to know his way around the greatest
library in the world.

7.
Angle of approach

At the end of the last chapter we made what we might call an aerial reconnaissance of the whole Bible, getting a quick glimpse of its general outline as we flew past. Keeping that picture, we could say that we are now approaching the moment of landing, when we want to make safe and satisfying contact with the territory we have identified. Having gathered so much background information, can we now plunge straight in? Certainly not, any more than a well-informed pilot will fling his plane recklessly down on the runway without paying careful attention to his approach and landing instructions!

This is a useful (if not perfect) illustration of the fact that there is a correct 'angle of approach' to the reading and study of the Bible, one made up of clear and important principles which the Christian will need to follow carefully if he is to derive maximum benefit from this marvellous book. In this chapter, we will take a brief look at these factors, which taken together form a composite answer to the question, 'How should I come to my Bible?'

Come to it regularly

We have already seen that the Bible describes itself as food for the soul, and this picture alone should be enough to show us the need of a regular intake. Yet the sad fact is that many people, professing Christians among them, treat the Bible as if it were no more than some kind of spiritual medicine cabinet, only to be opened when they feel in need of a spiritual pick-me-up. But that is a totally wrong approach. The Bible is *food*, not medicine, something that is meant to be taken as an everyday diet, and not just in emergency doses. This is precisely the picture Peter has in mind when he urges us to 'crave pure spiritual milk, so that by it you may grow up in your salvation' (1 Peter 2:2, 3). Growing up is a *natural* process, not something to be brought about by special treatment. When Paul was leaving Ephesus he told the elders of the church there, 'Now I commit you to God and to the word of his grace, which can build you up' (Acts 20:32), and again the picture is one of continuous nourishment, not an occasional 'shot in the arm'.

But we can put this another way. Surely we only have to be realistic and honest with ourselves to know how regularly we need to turn to the Bible? How often do we face problems, temptation and pressure? *Every day*! Then how often do we need instruction, guidance and greater encouragement? *Every day*! To catch all of these felt needs up into an even greater issue, how often do we need to see God's face, hear his voice, feel his touch, know his power? The answer to all of these questions is the same: *every day*! As the American evangelist D. L. Moody put it, 'A man can no more take in a supply of grace for the future than he can eat enough for the next six months, or take sufficient air into his lungs at one time to sustain life for a week. We must draw upon God's boundless store of grace from day to day as we need it.'

Come to it gratefully

This follows on from what we have just seen, because it

takes up Moody's point about 'God's boundless store of grace'. The Bible is not to be treated either as a computer, coldly housing thousands of religious facts, nor as a theological textbook, grimly demanding that we learn its contents as if we were preparing for an examination. Instead, it is a *means of grace,* part of God's loving provision for his children. The apostle James says that 'Every good and perfect gift is from above, coming down from the Father of the heavenly lights' (James 1:17) and of none of God's gifts is this more obviously true than of the Bible. There are so many parts of Scripture that teach this, but let us settle for this one classic passage from the Psalms, part of which was quoted in an earlier chapter: 'The law of the Lord is perfect, reviving the soul. The statutes of the Lord are trustworthy, making wise the simple. The precepts of the Lord are right, giving joy to the heart. The commands of the Lord are radiant, giving light to the eyes. The fear of the Lord is pure, enduring for ever. The ordinances of the Lord are sure and altogether righteous. They are more precious than gold, than much pure gold; they are sweeter than honey, than honey from the comb. By them is your servant warned; in keeping them there is great reward' (Psalm 19:7-11). Just go through those words again, and notice that the Bible is said to be God's means of providing man with spiritual energy, wisdom, joy, understanding, stability, truth, security and, as the result of his obedience to it, 'great reward'. Surely those are reasons enough for coming to it gratefully? As Robert Horn writes, 'God has favoured us with his autobiography in order that we might know and think his thoughts in every department of our lives.' That being so, we should no more come to the Bible without giving God thanks for his Word than we should come to the table without giving him thanks for our food. Come to the Bible gratefully! In Paul's words, 'Let the word of [God] dwell in you richly . . . *with gratitude in your hearts to God*' (Colossians 3:16).

Come to it diligently

This really links in with our first point about regularity.
For all that we have seen about the Bible as a means of
grace, God's gift to man, effective Bible study requires
discipline and diligence. Salvation is through faith, but
knowledge of the Bible is by works. The Bible is the
Christian's spiritual food, but it is not handed to him on
a plate!

Perhaps it is at this point that somebody might raise
questions about when we should study the Bible each
day, and for what length of time. The simple answer to
these questions is that there is no simple answer to these
questions! For instance, there is nothing hyper-spiritual
about studying for hours very early in the morning or
very late at night, though for some people this may be
the right thing to do, and younger Christians especially
should learn from history that all God's giants have been
men with enormous appetites for Scripture. Perhaps the
simplest thing to say is that each individual Christian
should take his own particular circumstances into consideration — age, state of health, school commitments,
working hours and family responsibilities, and so on.
These are the kinds of factors to be weighed in deciding
the right time and the right amount of time as far as you
are concerned — though, of course, I am not suggesting
that you should put all of the other factors first and then
give God what is left! For some, the ideal balance may
be fifteen minutes of prayer and Bible reading first thing
in the morning and a longer period of prayer and Bible
study at some time in the evening. Some may put these
the other way round. Others may find that an extended
time of study is only possible once or twice a week. Whatever the other permutations, a brief time of prayer and
meditation at the beginning of the day ought to be possible
for most people, and 'No Bible, no breakfast' would be a

good motto for every Christian — as long as that is not interpreted as meaning that you should miss both! But there are no rules here, and to hedge your Bible reading around with detailed regulations about hours and minutes will only succeed in turning a blessing into a burden. The time that is right for you is the time that proves best for you.

Having said that, it does not mean that you should feel free to do as you please. There is an element of duty in Bible-reading, for if God has deigned to speak, surely we have a responsibility to listen? If God has committed that word to writing, surely we must take time to read it, whatever disciplines that might mean for us? This point was powerfully made by Jim Elliot, one of the 'mid-century martyrs' who was put to death by the Auca Indians on the banks of the Curaray River in Ecuador in 1956. In his diary he wrote, 'I find I must drive myself to study, following the "ought" of conscience to gain anything at all from the Scripture, lacking any desire at times. It is important to learn respect and obedience to the "inner must" if godliness is to be a state of soul with me. I may no longer depend on pleasant impulses to bring me before the Lord. I must rather respond to principles I know to be right, whether I feel them to be enjoyable or not.'[1] Every sensitive Christian will understand that kind of language, and recognize its truth.

Come to it dependently

This is vitally important, and especially at this point, because without it, it might seem that I am suggesting a Bible-reading success formula that reads 'time + effort = blessing'. Yet that would be a dangerous delusion. No amount of time and effort spent studying the Bible will *automatically* produce the desired result. In a sense partially true of any book, but uniquely true of the Bible, only the author can explain its meaning. In his book *Faith that makes sense*, Dr J. Edwin Orr illustrates this on a human level by relating an incident during a mission he conducted at Seattle Pacific College. Walking along a corridor one day, he overheard three students arguing in a dormitory over a theological point he had made in one of his books. 'I'll tell you what Orr teaches,' one of them began, and then gave his explanation. As soon as he had finished, a second student gave his opinion, which was quite different. 'Pipe down everyone,' said the third student, '*I'll* tell you what Orr teaches.' Only when this third opinion had been offered did Dr Orr go into the room, and proceed to tell them exactly what he *did* mean!

As far as the Bible is concerned, it provides us with its own illustrations of the same truth. It is Luke who tells us the delightful story of the risen Christ meeting with the disciples on the road to Emmaus, and how '*he explained to them* what was said in all the Scriptures concerning himself' (Luke 24:27). Thinking it through later, the disciples spoke of Christ having '*opened the Scriptures* to us' (Luke 24:32). In the same chapter, Luke tells us that when Jesus met with eleven of the disciples at Jerusalem, he again reminded them of the Old Testament prophecies concerning the death of the Messiah, and '*opened their minds* so they could understand the Scriptures' (Luke 24:45). Notice the twin truths here. Only the Lord could open the Scriptures to their minds, and their minds to the Scriptures; and unless he had done so they would have remained clueless as to what the resurrection was all about, *even though Jesus was standing in front of them*! Nothing could more vividly illustrate our complete dependence on God himself to make his Word meaningful to us. In Paul's own words, 'No one knows the thoughts of God except the Spirit of God' (1 Corinthians 2:11). This is precisely why his constant

prayer for the Christians at Ephesus was 'that the God of
our Lord Jesus Christ, the glorious Father, may give you
the Spirit of wisdom and revelation, so that you may
know him better' (Ephesians 1:17), and why his great
concern for the Colossians was exactly the same: '. . . asking God to fill you with the knowledge of his will through
all spiritual wisdom and understanding' (Colossians 1:9).

Note all of this carefully, and whenever you open your
Bible remember that neither intelligence, nor experience,
nor diligence can produce a spiritual understanding of its
meaning. Your need of revelation is *total*, and that revelation can only come from God himself.

Come to it prayerfully

Again, the link is natural and obvious. If a person thinks
that he can read the Bible just as he would read any other
book, and understand its meaning simply by using his own
intelligence or common sense, then of course he will feel
no need to pray for God's help as he reads. But to approach
the Bible without prayer for this divine enabling is nothing
short of high-handed arrogance. It is an implicit denial of
God's sovereign claim that 'As the heavens are higher than
the earth, so are my ways higher than your ways and my
thoughts than your thoughts' (Isaiah 55:9).

John Owen, who was at one time spiritual adviser to
Oliver Cromwell and who has been described as the greatest
British theologian of all time, once wrote, 'For a man to
undertake the interpretation of any part or portion of
Scripture in a solemn manner, without *invocation of God*
to be taught and instructed by his Spirit, is a high provoca-
tion of him; nor shall I expect the discovery of truth from
anyone who so proudly and ignorantly engageth in a work
so much above his ability to manage.' The language may
be slightly old-fashioned and typically 'wordy', but the

point is clear. The same applies to another comment
he made at the same time: 'I suppose, therefore, this may
be fixed on as a *common principle of Christianity,* namely,
that constant and fervent prayer for the divine assistance
of the Holy Spirit is such an indispensable means for the
attaining of the knowledge of the mind of God in the
Scripture as that without it all others will not be available.'
The Christian who grasps the truth of those words, and
who realizes that without the illumination of the Holy
Scriptures by the Holy Spirit he will always be left
floundering in the dark, will always come to the Bible on
his knees.

This is certainly the *biblical* approach, because it is one
which claims a biblical promise, follows a biblical example
and obeys a biblical command. The promise is this: ' . . . if
you call out for insight and cry aloud for understanding,
and if you look for it as for silver and search for it as for
hidden treasure, then you will understand the fear of the
Lord and find the knowledge of God' (Proverbs 2: 3–5).
The example comes in words which many Christians use
literally as they come to their daily Bible reading: 'Open
my eyes that I may see wonderful things in your law'
(Psalm 119:18). The command is inescapable, because
everybody meets the qualification: 'If any of you lacks
wisdom, he should ask God, who gives generously to all
without finding fault; and it will be given to him' (James
1:5). Incidentally, notice that as well as issuing the command, James repeats the promise. But he also goes on to
add a very important condition: 'But when he asks, *he
must believe* and not doubt . . .' (James 1:6). Biblical
prayer is what James elsewhere describes as 'the prayer
offered in faith' (James 5:15), the kind of prayer that
confidently expects an answer, and it is this kind of faith
that should characterize your approach to the Bible. In
his powerful little book *The Pursuit of God,* A. W. Tozer
puts it like this: 'If you would follow on to know the

Lord, come at once to the open Bible *expecting it to speak to you.* Do not come with the notion that it is a *thing* which you may push around at your convenience. It is more than a thing, it is a voice, a word, the very word of the Living God.'[2]

Come to it submissively

Once again, this ties in exactly with what has gone before. The person with a deep conviction that the Bible is 'the very Word of the living God' will come to it as to no other book. He will not approach it casually or carelessly, nor will he study it coldly or clinically. Instead he will seek to come to it with his mind already reverently submitted to every part of its teaching. In his Preface to the Great Bible, published in 1539, Thomas Cranmer wrote, 'Wherefore I would advise you all that come to the reading or hearing of this book, which is the Word of God, the most precious jewel, the most holy relic that remaineth upon earth, that you bring with you the fear of God.' This, of course, is the real heart of the matter. We are to submit to the book because we worship the God who caused it to be written. What is more, our conviction that God speaks in *all* the Scriptures will mean that we will submit to every part of them.

The Bible itself has an excellent illustration of the right approach to hearing God's Word, in the story of the conversion of Cornelius, a Roman army officer. Already a God-fearing man, he was told by an angel to send for Simon Peter. Four days later, when Peter arrived at his home in Caesarea, Cornelius gathered his relatives and close friends, explained to Peter why he had sent for him and then said, 'Now we are all here in the presence of God to listen to everything the Lord has commanded you to tell us' (Acts 10:33). Read those

words through again, and notice how perfectly they illustrate the point of submission. Cornelius recognized that
he was to hear the *voice of God*, not just that of a man;
he was prepared to listen to *everything* God said, and not
just some things; and he accepted God's Word as a *com-
mandment*, not merely as a comment. Put yourself in the
place of Cornelius and his guests, and all the Bible's writers
in the place of Peter, and you have the perfect application
of the story. Come to the Bible submissively! Ask God to
open your heart, your mind, your conscience and your
will to every part of its truth. Stand under it even when
you cannot understand it. Submit yourself to all of its
doctrines, all of its disciplines and all of its demands. Far
from producing grim-faced drudgery or spineless apathy,
this approach is one which God has specifically promised
to honour: 'This is the one I esteem: he who is humble
and contrite in spirit, and trembles at my word' (Isaiah
66:2). This trembling is not the cringing fear of a terrified slave, wondering where the next blow is going to
fall; it is the reverent wonder of the believer who realizes
the tingling truth that whenever he opens his Bible to
read, God opens his mouth to speak. This is why the
psalmist who wrote, 'My heart trembles at your word'
(Psalm 119:161) could add in the very next breath,
'I *rejoice* in your promise like one who finds great spoil'
(Psalm 119:162). Submission to God's Word is not limiting, but liberating, because it moves a man into the wide
open spaces of God's promised blessing.

These, then, are some of the most important principles
to follow when approaching the Bible, and because they
are interwoven with each other, rather than shut up in
self-contained compartments, it might be helpful to summarize them in one paragraph. Come to the Bible *regularly*,
because there is not a single day in your life when it is not
relevant. Come to it *gratefully*, remembering that it is
part of God's gracious provision for you. Come to it

diligently, accepting that genuine Bible study will mean discipline and effort. Come to it *prayerfully*, specifically asking for the help of the Holy Spirit to enable you to understand its true meaning. Come to it *submissively*, accepting its absolute authority in every part of your life.

Thomas Watson once said, 'Think in every line you read that God is speaking to you.' Perhaps that can serve to summarize our summary, because the man who does so will surely follow the principles we have examined, and in doing so he will have the right angle of approach.

8.
Methods and means

If they were to be absolutely honest, I wonder how many Christians would have to admit that their personal Bible reading is far from satisfactory? In spite of their genuine belief that the Bible is the Word of God, and is 'living and active' (Hebrews 4:12), the sad truth of the matter is that for them it seems at times to be deadly dull. Believing it to be divinely inspired, they find it decidedly uninspiring.

There may be more than one reason for this, and for anyone who suspects that the cause may be spiritual, I would suggest a very careful reading of Luke 8:4—15. Notice that the fault lay in the soil, not in the seed. If there is work to be done there, then set to and do it! For others, however, the cause may be more practical, and for some it is simply lack of disciplined effort. It has been said that 'The Bible does not yield its riches to casual prospectors, but to conscientious, methodical miners who dig deep and take trouble.' To switch to a picture we have already used several times, the Bible describes itself as food, but we are not to think of it as a spiritual supermarket, with the proprietor inviting us to wander casually around picking up any bits and pieces that take our fancy. To do that is to dishonour the God who caused it to be written 'rule on rule, rule on rule' (Isaiah 28:10).

Others may be getting nowhere because their Bible reading has no order or shape, no structure or aim. They flit around from place to place looking for 'blessed thoughts' or 'precious promises', but find no real satisfaction. Then there are others who have followed one method of Bible study for so long that the whole business has degenerated from the methodical to the mechanical, and now has no sense of adventure, progress or achievement. Yet all of these are tragic situations, because the Bible is not only wonderfully rich in the variety of its content, it also lends itself to many different methods of reading and study. What is more, there has never been a time in all history when there have been so many excellent aids to Bible study at the Christian's disposal.

In this chapter I want to suggest eight different methods of Bible study, and at the same time to mention some of the means of help that are available. Perhaps the only other word of introduction necessary is to say that I am writing with personal rather than group study in mind. Some of the methods are obviously adaptable for group use, but they are basically intended for the individual Christian.

1. From cover to cover

The American evangelist R. A. Torrey once wrote, 'The whole Bible is the Word of God, therefore the whole Bible should be studied. Men become insufferable cranks by confining their Bible study to single books or to a narrow circle of topics.' A good point, and, strange as it may seem, many Christians have missed one of the most obvious methods of covering the whole Bible, which is to read it right through from beginning to end. To some who have never done this, being asked to wade through the whole Bible from Genesis to Revelation may sound like being sentenced to a long stretch of hard labour, but it can in fact be an exhilarating experience. Even more important, it is the most natural way to get a complete overall picture of everything that God's Word has to say. G. H. Lang, a

well-known figure among the Christian Brethren until his
death in 1958, provides a good illustration of this in his
autobiography *An Ordered Life*. He says that he was converted at the age of seven, but by the time he was twenty-
three he had only read the Bible 'desultorily' (a healthy
piece of honesty there!). With delightful simplicity he
goes on, 'It occurred to me that perhaps I had not read it
all and therefore *there might be things my God and Father
wished to say to me that I did not know*. Obviously the
simple cure for this was to read it straight through.'[1] He did
so in five months. When he reached 1 Corinthians 2:10–12
he realized for the first time that 'the Author of the Book,
the Spirit of truth, was with me to open to me even the
deep mysteries of God . . . It was as if a pupil should have
as tutor the writer of the textbook used.' From then on,
he began to study the Bible 'with confidence and resolution'. Since the Old Testament was longer than the New,
he decided to read them side by side, not returning to
Genesis until he had read Malachi, but going back to
Matthew as soon as he reached the end of Revelation. He
felt that his method was not only simple and comprehensive, but it had the advantage that 'every topic of Scripture
is considered in the proportion assigned to it by the Holy
Spirit, and the student thus surveys each topic as often
and as long as it is found in the Bible'. That is typical of
G. H. Lang – and very difficult to contradict! Later in life
he went through his daily consecutive reading in English,
Greek and German!

But how will a right-through-the-Bible reading scheme
work out in practice? This will obviously depend on how
much is read each day. Let us look at a few examples,
taking Lang's method first. Assuming you read three Old
Testament and three New Testament chapters a day, you
would get through the Old Testament in just over ten
months and the New Testament in just under three months.
Put another way, in one year you would have read the

New Testament four times, and be somewhere in Numbers the second time through the Old. Another straightforward system for reading the Bible through in a year would be to read three chapters on every weekday and five on Sundays. That would get you home with four or five days to spare. Stepping up the pace, I know of a Christian who reads ten chapters a day: two each in the Old and New Testaments, five in the Psalms and one in Proverbs. In this way he goes through the Old Testament once a year, the New Testament three times a year, and the Psalms and Proverbs once a month. Robert Murray M'Cheyne worked out a simple scheme that in the course of a year covered the New Testament and Psalms twice and the rest of the Bible once, arranging the readings into sections for family and private use. The whole scheme, including his notes on how best to use it, is now published as a very helpful leaflet by The Banner of Truth Trust under the title *M'Cheyne's Calendar for Daily Readings*. Another simple calendar to guide the reader through the Bible in the course of a year is *Light on my Path*, published by the Evangelical Movement of Wales.

These are some suggestions. If necessary, have a 'trial run' to find out how much it is sensible for you to read each day. Then, having fixed on this, *let nothing deflect you from doing it*. Be disciplined, and determine not to turn excuses into reasons. Having said that, I do not mean that you should be satisfied with just ploughing through your 'quota' for the day. Although this is Bible *reading* rather than Bible *study*, the all-important thing is that it is the *Bible* that is being read and you should be praying and expecting that God will speak to you through it as you read. Even in this general approach, have a notebook handy, and at the end of your reading jot down any points that have made a particular impression: a doctrinal truth, a promise, a warning, a command; a passage, word, phrase or verse to be studied at some other time. A loose-leaf notebook would enable you to keep this material in logical order. In this way, reading the Bible through will not only bring its own immediate rewards, it will open the way to endless possibilities in other areas.

Though I am not suggesting that this should be your permanent or only form of Bible intake, there are those who would say that it has proved of continuous blessing. I once met a man who was enthusiastically reading his Bible through for the forty-first time, and heard of another who had read it through twice a year for all twenty-six years of his Christian life; both found it as fresh as ever. At the time he wrote his autobiography, G. H. Lang had followed his scheme for fifty years and had not felt 'the need or advantage of any other scheme or arrangement of Bible reading',[2] while George Muller, the famous Christian philanthropist, is said to have read his Bible through 200 times in the last twenty-five years of his life. The Christian who has never read his Bible through even *once* is obviously missing something!

2. A book at a time

Archdeacon T. C. Hammond used to advise young Christians to 'read the Bible in great dollops'. What that lacked in elegance it certainly made up in eloquence — and it remains good advice for Christians of all ages. One of the most natural and helpful ways of doing this is to try to get a good overall grasp of the Bible one book at a time. After all, as that is the way it was written, surely it is one of the obvious ways in which it should be read? What I have in mind here is not a phrase-by-phrase study (we shall come to that in a moment) but rather getting hold of a general outline of a whole book so that its main message is fixed firmly in the mind. In his *Survey of the Bible*, William Hendriksen says, 'When anyone mentions

Galatians, the student of the Bible should be able, without the least hesitation, to give theme and outline.' If that leaves you gasping, perhaps we have already hit on a 'must' as far as you are concerned! Incidentally, one of the fringe benefits of this kind of study is that the more familiar verses are seen in their proper context, with the result that their importance becomes so much clearer. To illustrate from Galatians: many Christians would be able to quote (more or less accurately!) Paul's famous words, 'I no longer live, but Christ lives in me . . .' (Galatians 2:20), and could also manage at least part of 'But the fruit of the Spirit is love, joy, peace . . .' (Galatians 5:22), but how many could put those great truths into their right context? Yet they were written in context, and not just thrown in when Paul had special bursts of inspiration!

Then how do you go about this method? The first thing to do is to read a book right through. Secondly, read it through again. Thirdly, read it through again . . . and so on! The number of times you will need to do this will partly depend on the length and nature of the book — Exodus is not quite as easy to grasp as 3 John! You may want to read it through in different translations — even a paraphrased version might be helpful in getting the general drift of the larger books — but remember my earlier advice about concentrating on the one version you believe is the best for you. One thing that may surprise you is how quickly some books can be read, many of them, of course, at one sitting. Take Ephesians, for instance. Someone has said that it contains 'some of the most sublime thought, pious exhortation, affectionate admonition, depth of doctrine and animated fervour of style to be found in the New Testament'; it is so packed with truth that the original version of William Gurnall's *The Christian in Complete Armour*, a commentary on just eight verses in chapter 6, ran to 877 pages; yet the whole epistle can be read in just ten minutes. Surely that should whet your appetite?

At least to begin with, read the book through *without* any Bible study helps. Try to get your *own* 'feel' of the book. Which section is it in — history, prophecy, poetry, doctrinal? What seems to be its main purpose? Is there an outline emerging as you become familiar with it? If so, sketch it down, shaping it as you go along. Are there any words or phrases that keep cropping up? If so, underline them and draw another line linking them together, or put a cross-reference in the margin, or jot them down in a loose-leaf notebook. For instance, if you were reading Philippians in the NIV you would come across the word 'joy' in 1:4; 1:25; 1:26; 2:2; 2:29 and 4:1, and the word 'rejoice' in 1:18 (twice); 2:17; 2:18; 3:1; 4:4 (twice) and 4:10. These references alone would give you a clue that although it was written from prison (see 1:7, 13, 14) one of its main themes is that in Christ the Christian can triumph over all adversity. You would, of course, come across more or less the same words in any other version. This is admittedly a very simple example, and many other books, particularly in the Old Testament, will not be as straightforward. But every one can be prised open eventually, and the rewards will always be worth the effort. Yet remember that at this level, too, your purpose is not just knowledge but nourishment. Aim to take in food, not just facts. Apply the truths you discover to your own heart and life, and be open to God's correction, instruction and direction.

Having tried to get your best understanding of what the book is saying, now is the time to check with a reference book of some kind, such as a Bible handbook or commentary, to see how the book is outlined there. The comparisons may be interesting! Having done this, try to boil the outline down to essentials that you can jot down on a single page of your notebook, or in the margin of your Bible, or even to commit to memory. I firmly believe that for Christians who have never done it before, this kind of outline study could be a real breakthrough in their grasp of what the Bible is saying. Try it, and see what I mean!

3. Into the text

Logically, we ought now to look at the kind of study that takes us through a book more slowly and at greater depth. Here, the list of helps is almost endless, and for this very reason let me give a word of advice and encouragement before mentioning even one of them. That word is this: never forget that God can communicate the deepest truths of his Word directly to the heart of the simplest believer without any human help. The Holy Spirit does not need the help of clergymen to get the message across, nor is he dependent on the efforts of the experts. Whatever use you make of aids to Bible study, let your *primary* dependence be on God himself, who 'guides the humble in what is right and teaches them his way' (Psalm 25:9). Having said that, recognize that among God's gracious gifts to the church are 'pastors and teachers' (Ephesians 4:11), men called by God to devote themselves to the study of the Scriptures and related subjects in a special way and equipped to share the results of their work for the benefit of the whole church. No sensible Christian will totally refuse the benefit of their ministry.

The first of the helps we could mention are dated Bible reading notes prepared by a number of Christian organizations, and usually designed for the kind of devotional study that comes somewhere between the outline approach that we have just looked at and the detailed study we shall come on to in a moment. The best-known of these are by Scripture Union and include the little booklets *Daily Bread* and *Daily Notes*, issued quarterly. The comments in *Daily Bread* are very brief, basic and devotional, while those in *Daily Notes* are the same size but written at a slightly deeper level. In the same general category is my own *Read Mark Learn* (Evangelical Press), containing forty-five undated studies in the Gospel of Mark, originally prepared for new converts but suitable for more general use. *Food for Life* (IVP) is sub-titled 'Personal Bible study made appetizing' and is an excellent little book to have on hand, not only for its worked-out examples of different methods of Bible study (based on the RSV) but for a great amount of sensible advice on the whole subject in general.

Moving on to fuller notes, my own *Luke Comes Alive!* (Evangelical Press) might be a suitable introduction. In it, I have gone through the Gospel of Luke in sixty-two sections and have deliberately aimed at drawing people from 'hit and run' (and often 'hit and miss') Bible reading into a more satisfying approach. An eight-part series, *Understanding the Old Testament* and a ten-part series *Understanding the New Testament* (both Scripture Union) present the same material as their twenty-part series *Bible Study Books*. These cover the whole Bible over a period of five years. The material is also available in four case-bound volumes entitled *Daily Bible Commentary*.

We then come on to Bible commentaries, books aimed at dealing with the text in greater detail. Too many Christians make the mistake of thinking that commentaries are only for use by preachers and teachers, but nothing is further from the truth, and wise use of a good commentary can be a tremendous help to the 'ordinary' Christian. Of the commentaries that cover the whole Bible in one volume, one of the most widely used is *Matthew Henry's Commentary* (Marshall, Morgan and Scott), an abridged version of a work originally produced in seven volumes and still available in a three-volume edition.

Matthew Henry, a Nonconformist minister, began writing his commentary in 1704, but died ten years later before the work was completed. The last section (Romans–Revelation) was later written by fourteen like-minded men, using Matthew Henry's unfinished notes. This superb commentary has been recognized as a spiritual classic for over 250 years, and Matthew Henry's sparkling comments still break through the 'olde-worlde' English in which they were written and the AV text on which they were based. A more modern one is *The New Bible Commentary Revised* (IVP). Based on the RSV, it is the work of over fifty contributors and, as well as a commentary on each book in the Bible, contains special articles on several important subjects, including the Bible's revelation, inspiration and authority.

Now published in three volumes, *Matthew Poole's Commentary on the Holy Bible* (The Banner of Truth Trust) was originally issued as a two-volume work in 1685, and, interestingly enough, was also completed after his death by the commentator's friends. Matthew Poole lacks Matthew Henry's sparkle, but he is quite readable and extremely helpful. C. H. Spurgeon said that if he could have only one commentary, having already read Henry, he would probably choose Poole, adding, 'You meet with no ostentation of learning in Poole, and that for the simple reason that he was so profoundly learned as to be able to give results without a display of his intellectual crockery.'

Next we come to a series of commentaries, in which each volume usually covers just one book in the Bible. Of those available today, the *Tyndale Commentaries* (IVP) are very helpful for general use. The New Testament is covered in twenty volumes and the Old Testament series is well under way. All the volumes in the New Testament are based on the AV, except for the last to be published (Luke) which switches to the RSV. In the Old Testament series, the authors base their work more loosely on several versions. Handy in size, and pitched at a level that many people will be able to understand perfectly well, the Tyndale Commentaries have been widely acclaimed. Finally, we come to the real heavyweights. *The Geneva Series of Commentaries* (The Banner of Truth Trust), a magnificent, ongoing production at present covering about thirty of the Bible's books. Although many are reprints of older works (John Calvin on Genesis was first published in 1554) and some are fairly hefty in size (John Brown takes 1,227 pages to cover 1 Peter!) they are all the products of fine scholarship and warm-hearted devotion, and are not only a 'must' for preachers and teachers, but an excellent investment for the serious Bible student. They are possibly without equal in their field. If you are a newcomer to this league, I would suggest that you begin with one of the New Testament volumes by William Hendriksen, a thorough, modern commentator whose work is excellent.

So much for the commentaries, but let me add a word of advice. Beware of getting 'hooked' on them — and in particular of getting chained to any one man's interpretation of Scripture. Bible study is not meant to be a spectator sport, in which you just sit and watch what someone else does with the text. Rather, it is meant to be your own direct encounter with God's Word. An old lady was once asked whether she used commentaries in her Bible study. 'Yes', she replied, 'I like to read them sometimes. I find that the Bible throws a great deal of light on them!' There is nothing I can add to that!

4. One word only

One of the most fascinating methods of Bible study is to concentrate for a time on just one word. This kind of study also makes a great deal of sense, because once we have tracked down every occasion on which the Bible uses a particular word, and have understood its meaning in its context, we will have clearly established that word's own importance in the Bible. What is more, as we shall see later, the study of single words opens the way into an even wider field, the study of whole themes or subjects.

However, as soon as we try to tackle the study of individual words we come up against a major problem: in many cases several different words in Hebrew and Greek are translated by one word in English, and in many other cases one word in the original language is translated several different ways in ours. Then what hope is there for the ordinary Christian with no knowledge of Hebrew or Greek? The answer is a *concordance*, a reference book which lists in alphabetical order the words used in our English Bible. But to solve the first part of our problem (several original words becoming one in English) it needs to be an *analytical* concordance, one which shows us which original word is being translated. And to solve the second part of our problem (one original word translated in different ways) it also needs to have an index of the original words and an indication of which English words have been used to translate them.

The book which does all of these things is the *Analytical Concordance to the Bible* (Lutterworth Press). Originally published in 1879, and compiled by Robert Young, a printer's apprentice who became a theologian and missionary, it is perhaps the most indispensable piece of 'machinery' any student of the Bible could possess. To begin with, it lists every word in the Bible in alphabetical order — about 311,000 references in all. It then arranges them in groups according to which Hebrew, Greek, or in some cases Aramaic word was used in the original, and gives the literal meaning of each of these words. Finally, it has 'index-lexicons' to the Old and New Testaments, listing the original words in alphabetical order, showing which English words have been used to translate them, and how many times each of the English words has been used.

With this wonderful tool, you can now get to work. Let us see what happens. Perhaps during your 'outline' study of a New Testament book, you come across an important word you want to study in depth. Firstly, you look it up in the concordance. How many times does it occur? Let us say a total of twenty, five in the Old Testament and fifteen in the New. In the Old Testament group, it is the same Hebrew word that is translated each time, and the literal meaning shows it to be right in line with the word you are studying. Fine, but what about the New Testament? Of the fifteen references, let us say that five translate a totally different word in the original Greek, and can therefore be 'dropped'. You are now left with fifteen references, five in the Old Testament and ten in the New. Now is the time to look them up in your Bible, read them through, try to grasp the context, and make any notes you think are important at this point. Now look back to the original Hebrew word in the concordance (this is transliterated into English letters) and look this word up in the Old Testament Index-Lexicon. Is it translated into any other English words? In addition, are there any words which obviously come from the same root? If so, how are these translated into English? A note of all of this, then back to the main part of the concordance to discover their whereabouts in the Bible. Now on to the Bible to read all these verses through, get the context, make notes and think through what these scriptures mean. In particular, apply all of this truth to your own life; remember that the purpose of Bible study is to grow saints, not encyclopaedias! Finally, you still have your original Greek word to check. Back to the concordance! What was the original Greek word? Look it up in the index-lexicon. Has it been translated in any other ways? . . . And so on, as before — including the notes, the meditation and the application of it all to your heart and life.

I hope that does not sound too complicated! There is not space here to give a worked-out example, but I am sure that you will not find word study difficult if you carefully follow the directions I have given. All I can say is that I have found this particular kind of study totally absorbing, and my battered concordance almost 'unputdownable' at times. I firmly believe that if you start getting to grips with this method you will begin to enjoy your Bible as never before. Incidentally, 'Young's' is based on the AV, but if you are using another version of the Bible there is no real problem; you simply use the AV as a 'bridge' between that version and the concordance. For example, if you came to 1 Corinthians 3:1 in the NIV and wanted to study the word 'worldly', you would turn to the AV, discover that the word used there is 'carnal', turn up that word in the concordance, and then follow the method I have explained.

There are a number of other concordances available, two very good ones being *Cruden's Complete Concordance* (Lutterworth Press) and Strong's *The Exhaustive Concordance of the Bible* (published by Macdonald and distributed in Great Britain by Evangelical Press) — but none is better than 'Young's' and for the Bible student who means business this ought to be a classic case of 'only the best is good enough'. *The NIV Complete Concordance* (Hodder and Stoughton) was published in 1983, but has no Hebrew or Greek lexicons.

Perhaps this would be as good a place as any to say something about the cost of providing oneself with aids to Bible study — a point that may have already entered your mind! The first thing to say is that different people will clearly have different needs; for instance, I would not expect a ninety-year-old to begin setting up an extensive library with the same enthusiasm as someone in his twenties. Age, ability to study, financial position and other factors will obviously have a bearing here. However, there is no doubt that many Christians have much too little in the way of solid aids to Bible study while their shelves are crammed with the 'experience' books that are currently flooding the Christian market. Yet this imbalance is tragic— a diet of second-hand thrills is no substitute for books that will enrich your life by opening up the treasures of God's Word. Finally, is Christian literature *really* expensive when compared with other things? For example, a good edition of *Young's Concordance* costs about the same as the petrol needed for 400 miles of driving in an average-sized car. A Tyndale Commentary works out at no more than a modest meal in an ordinary restaurant. A commentary in the Geneva Series can be had for the same price as a long-playing record. It may well be that for many people, the real question is not 'What is the price?' but 'What is the priority?' We can usually afford the things we think most important. To look at all of this from another angle, it would not be difficult to prove that the price of good Christian books means that we are paying less than a penny an hour for the author's labour — and getting the work of the printer, publisher, distributor and retailer thrown in free! Is that really too much to ask? Think it over as we turn to look at some more methods and means.

5. Subject matters

Words, of course, are subjects in themselves, but, as we saw at the beginning of the last section, they lead naturally to other subjects or themes through the ideas that link them together. For example, a study of the word 'man' would be fascinating and helpful on its own, but if you began to jot down other related subjects as you were studying, think of some of the other avenues that would open up. You would not get very far before coming face to face with the fact of creation. That in turn would quickly lead you to the great overall subject of God, though perhaps you might want to concentrate on his sovereignty, or power, or love, as these are demonstrated so clearly in the creation story. On the other hand, you could not study 'man' for long without bumping into 'sin', and immediately you could go off in several directions. You could study the subject of temptation, which, of course, leads back to the devil; or within the general framework of sin, you could look at its nature, characteristics and effect; or you could look at the only remedy for sin, provided by Christ — and that leads on to subjects like atonement, grace, mercy, repentance, faith, forgiveness, and so on.

It is surely easy to see what a fascinating method of study this is, and most of all because all the Bible's teaching holds together in perfect unity. As somebody has rightly said, 'All Scripture is the context in the light of which any Scripture is to be considered and applied.' This means that going on to related subjects in the way shown above is not going off at a tangent so much as completing some other part of a perfect circle of divine truth. In a book of this size, there will not be room to develop the idea of studying themes or subjects any further. Instead, let me mention some of the tools that are available for the task.

Perhaps my own testimony will help here. When I became a Christian the first 'subject' book I used was R. T. Archibald's *The Spirit's Sword* (Scripture Union). This very simple series of twelve subjects is intended to cover a year of weekly studies, but if I remember rightly I was in a holy hurry to go places, and was soon looking

elsewhere for further help. I found it in *Every Man a Bible
Student*, by Joe Church (now published by Paternoster
Press), which outlined forty-four different themes, quoted
hundreds of verses to be looked up and made brief com-
ments at various points. I found it a great help at the time,
and the enlarged and revised version (now with forty-seven
themes and based on the RSV) could be useful as a brief
guide to some of the Bible's major themes. After that
I went through *In Understanding be Men* by T. C.
Hammond (IVP). Seven main sections cover Scripture,
The Godhead, Man and Sin, The Person and Work of Christ,
The Holy Spirit, The Corporate Life of the Christian and
The Last Things, and each section outlines the background
to the doctrine being covered, gives a selection of Scriptures
to be examined, asks several questions and lists other books
on the same subject. Although there is more reading
material here than encouragement to 'do it yourself', it is
still a helpful introduction.

Much more direct is *Questions on the Christian Faith
answered from the Bible*, by Derek Prime (Hodder and
Stoughton) a really first-class little book packed with
biblical data on fifty subjects and with an excellent appen-
dix of brief Bible definitions ranging from 'Adoption' to
'Wrath'.

One of the best outline books available today is *Summary of Christian Doctrine* by Louis Berkhof (The Banner
of Truth Trust). Superbly concise, it covers a vast amount
of ground in a sound and simple way. For Berkhof's full
treatment you have to go to his *Systematic Theology* (The
Banner of Truth Trust). Indexes to subjects and texts will
help you to find your way around, but do not buy it for
light reading! This kind of book certainly sorts out the
men from the boys — and surely helps many boys to
become men! In studying themes, a Bible dictionary can
be very useful, and *The New Bible Dictionary* (IVP) is a
positive mine of information, with articles on subjects

ranging from Aaron to Zuzim, and with seventeen full-colour maps among its additional features. Some Bibles have their own built-in system of cross-references, indexes and other helps in tracing subjects through. One of the most comprehensive is the *New Chain-Reference Bible* (B. B. Kirkbride Bible Co.). Its 'chain reference' system was devised by Frank Thompson, and other features include a 'text cyclopedia', Bible readings, outline studies of the Bible, character studies, an abbreviated concordance and a 12-page Bible atlas. An edition of the *New Chain Reference Bible* based on the text of the NIV was published in 1983.

Finally, of course, there is your concordance, and in studying themes you will find it indispensable, because at the end of the day the most direct helps are those which make it clear that the only ultimate means of studying the Bible is *the Bible itself*. Many Bible scholars have borne this out. William Gurnall wrote, 'Compare Scripture with Scripture. False doctrines, like false witnesses, agree not among themselves.' Dr A. T. Pierson put it like this: 'No investigation of Scripture, in its various parts and separate texts, however important, must impair the sense of the supreme value of its united witness. There is not a form of evil doctrine or practice that may not claim apparent sanction from isolated passages, but nothing erroneous or vicious can ever find countenance from the Word of God when the whole united testimony of Scripture is weighed against it. Partial examination will result in partial views of truth, which are necessarily imperfect. Only careful comparison will show the complete mind of God.' It is this truth above all that makes the study of Bible themes not just endlessly fascinating but enduringly rewarding.

6. Characters

Every communicator in the mass media today recognizes

the value of a 'human interest story'. Cold facts or statistics are all very well, but public interest really comes to life when this information is focused on human beings. All the world loves a love story. Most people are immediately attracted to tales of personal heroism, courage, dedication, sacrifice and success, and equally interested in stories of hardship, fear, pressure, injustice and failure.

This in-built factor ought to draw us naturally to another very profitable method of Bible study — a detailed look at some of the individual people mentioned in its pages. Needless to say, this opens up another enormous area of possibility. *Everyone in the Bible,* by William P. Barker (Oliphants) claims to name 'absolutely every man, woman and child — important or obscure — mentioned in the Bible', and the list comes to nearly 3,000, from Aaron to Zurishaddai, including all thirty Zechariahs! With Scripture references and brief outlines of whatever life story the Bible gives, this makes an excellent index to the whole subject.

Of course, not every person mentioned in the Bible is of equal importance, or equally profitable as the basis of a character study, though even a thumb-nail sketch can sometimes speak volumes. However, there is not a great deal to be gained by pondering at great length the significance of a gentleman by the name of Anub, because we are told nothing about him except that he was begotten by Coz somewhere in the middle of 1 Chronicles 4! On the other hand, what a tremendous array of great character studies the Bible does give us! Think for a moment of people like Adam, Noah, Abraham, Moses, Joseph, Jacob, Joshua, Gideon, Samuel and David in the Old Testament, or of Paul, Stephen, Peter, Luke and Timothy in the New Testament. Anti-heroes, too — people like Jeroboam, Uzziah, Jezebel, Judas Iscariot and Pontius Pilate — can be studied with real profit, helping us to avoid their sins and the tragedies that followed them. Many of these are mentioned in a series of sixteen little books entitled *Bible Characters and Doctrines* (Scripture Union). Based on the RSV, it is arranged to cover characters and doctrines alternatively over a period of four years, and each section has questions and themes for further study. For a more devotional approach, *Daily Thoughts on Bible Characters,* by Harry Foster (Victory Press) suggests a Bible reading and then gives a very perceptive meditation for each day of the year. The characters are arranged in alphabetical order, from Aaron on 1 January to Zerubbabel on 31 December, and the book is a lovely introduction to the value of character study.

To get some idea of the wealth of material available in the Bible for character study, let us glance at just one of the people mentioned a moment ago. Jacob's life story runs from Genesis 25–49. During this time he cheated his older brother and his dying father, ran for his life, promised to mend his ways after a remarkable vision, in which he saw angels commuting between heaven and earth, got married twice (to two sisters, and in the course of eight days!), tricked his father-in-law into handing over most of his livestock, had a remarkable encounter with God, returned home and made things up with his brother, suffered the horrors of having his daughter raped and his favourite son sold off to passing traders, settled down to a reformed family life and, when the country was hit by famine, emigrated to Egypt, where he died at something over 130 years of age. There seems to be a smattering of human interest there! But the real point is that there is much *more* than human interest. The story of Jacob is not only real and riveting, it is *relevant*, because like the rest of Scripture, it was 'written to teach us' (Romans 15:4). In studying the life of this man, who was by turn crafty, loving, bitter, devout, courageous, cowardly, prayerful and trusting, we can get a deep insight not only into human nature, but also into God's dealings with the fragile sinners we all are.

Perhaps that one illustration will whet your appetite and encourage you to include character study in your Bible-reading programme from time to time. Having decided on a character, begin by getting the background facts right. Who was he (or she, of course)? Where does this character fit into the Bible narrative? A Bible dictionary will come in useful here. When you have the answers to these questions, read all the passages in which the person concerned is mentioned (your concordance will be needed yet again). Next, as you get closer in, perhaps with the help of a commentary, use your notebook to build up your own 'Identikit' picture of the person concerned; their personality and characteristics, strengths and weaknesses. Finally, as with all other Bible study, apply what you learn to yourself. Ask *honestly* what God is saying to you about your own life — your home, your family, your relationships in the church or at work, your ambitions, your life-style, your Christian service and so on. Used in this way, character study can be both challenging and enriching.

7. The living Word

Martin Luther once wrote, 'As we go to the cradle only in order to find the baby, so we go to the Scriptures only to find Christ.' This was the great Reformer's way of fixing in the mind the great truth that Jesus Christ is the great central figure to whom the whole of Scripture points. To begin with, Christ is the key to a proper understanding of the Old Testament. He himself said of that entire body of writings, 'These are the Scriptures that testify *about me*' (John 5:39). He explained to the disciples on the road to Emmaus 'what was said in all the Scriptures *concerning himself*' (Luke 24:27) and later told another group of them, 'Everything must be fulfilled that is written *about me* in the law of Moses, the Prophets and the Psalms' (Luke 24:44). He is also, and obviously, the key to a proper understanding of the New Testament. The four Gospels are his biography; Acts was specifically written by Luke as a direct follow-up to 'all that Jesus began to do and to teach' (Acts 1:1); all of the epistles were written by and to people for whom Christ had become a living Saviour; and the last book in the Bible, for all its mystery, is clearly said to be 'the revelation of Jesus Christ' (Revelation 1:1). As the *New Bible Handbook* puts it, 'It is through the book that we know the Person, and because of the Person that we have received the book.'

All of this means that to study the person and work of Christ is a thoroughly *biblical* method of studying the Bible itself, because just as it is impossible to study the Bible thoroughly without building up a picture of Christ, so it is impossible to study the person of Christ in detail without discovering an outline of the whole body of God's revealed truth. It is no coincidence that both the Scriptures and Christ are called 'the Word of God' (Hebrews 4:12; Revelation 19:13). To study the Word of God is to discover Christ, and to study Christ is to discover the Word of God.

But how do you go about a study of Christ? The simple truth is that you can incorporate every one of the methods we have already examined, and use virtually all the means or aids we have mentioned. In addition, a work such as *Nave's Topical Bible* (Moody Press) might be helpful, with its detailed grouping and indexing of thousands of references. It is here especially that you will appreciate the value of some kind of loose-leaf system for note-taking, and of developing your own system for making cross-references in your Bible. Time and again, while studying in other areas, you will come across a reference to Christ, and will want to make a note of it for future use.

As far as specifically studying Christ is concerned, every word told about him is important, though there are obviously some aspects of his person and work that ought to be given special attention. You may want to draw up your own list of these as you go along, but here are some suggestions, put into four 'natural' groups: (1) His deity, eternity, glory and names or titles; (2) his birth, life, death, resurrection, ascension, second coming and fulfilment of prophecy; (3) his mission, teaching, parables, miracles, prayers and claims; (4) his humanity, holiness, love, meekness, humility and patience. Some of these obviously overlap, but you can easily work out your own method of dealing with the material. At the same time, never forget that the material is meant to be dealing with you! You should no more be content with classifying information about Christ than a thirsty man would be content with analysing the contents of a glass of water. In the service of the Lord's Supper laid down in the Book of Common Prayer, there is a point at which the minister hands the bread to the communicant with the lovely words: 'Take and eat this in remembrance that Christ died for thee, and *feed on him in thy heart by faith with thanksgiving*.' I cannot possibly think of a better way of receiving not only the sacrament in which he is remembered but also the Scriptures in which he is revealed. As you come to the Bible, and especially to those parts which speak directly and specifically of your Saviour, learn to feed on *him*, in your heart, by faith and with thanksgiving. Here is one of the great open secrets of how to 'grow in the grace and knowledge of our Lord and Saviour Jesus Christ' (2 Peter 3:18).

8. Remember, remember

There can be no question that the current deluge of different translations has been largely responsible for a serious decline in one of the most beneficial methods of getting to grips with the Bible's contents, namely memorization. It is a sad irony that so many commendable efforts to make its message more *widely* known have for many Christians resulted in its becoming less *well* known. Young Christians, in particular, while able to give the general drift of what the Bible says about certain things in general, are becoming less able to say *precisely* what the Bible says about anything in particular. Perhaps this is not surprising, because every year or so they are hit by an avalanche of advertising introducing yet another 'best ever' version. Duly impressed, they add it to their collection, often to find themselves more confused than ever as to which one they should use regularly. This is not meant to be a cynical dismissal of all modern translations – quantity, not quality is the problem here – and it is encouraging to read in the Preface to the NIV the translators' hope that 'the wide use of the New International Version will encourage the wholesome practice of memorizing Scripture'. One thing is certain: the first step to memorizing Scripture is to make an early choice, using the kind of criteria outlined in Chapter 5, of one basic translation, and *then keep to it.*

As to the value of memorizing, we can surely get very good evidence from the Bible itself. It is interesting to notice how often in the Old Testament the people of Israel were told to remember not only God's actions but his words, and it is perhaps no coincidence that on the very last page of the Old Testament God says, '*Remember* the law of my servant Moses, the decrees and laws I gave him at Horeb for all Israel' (Malachi 4:4). Then there is the example of Jesus in the wilderness, being tempted by the devil. He immediately countered each attack with the words: 'It is written . . .' followed by quotations from Deuteronomy (twice) and the Psalms (see Matthew 4:4, 6, 7) with no suggestion in the narrative that he needed time to look up the passages concerned! Or take Peter on the Day of Pentecost. When the crowd suggested that the apostles were drunk, he replied, 'No, this is what was spoken by the prophet Joel . . .' and promptly quoted a sizeable chunk from the writings of that 'minor prophet'. Stephen is another example. Given an opportunity to make a final speech before his execution, he gave a masterly summary of about a thousand years of Old Testament history, inserting quotations from Genesis, Exodus, Deuteronomy, Amos and Isaiah as he went along (see Acts 7:1–53). How many Christians could manage that today?

Yet Bible memorization ought to be easier now than it was then because at that time there was no reference system of chapters and verses. Paul would have had no idea what you meant by 'Isaiah 53:6' and Peter could not have told you what '2 Chronicles 7:14' was to save his life! The division of the text of the Bible into chapters and verses has had a complicated history, but the final touches (the present New Testament verses) were applied in 1551 by a French publisher called Robert Estienne (otherwise known as Robert Stephanus). Looked at as a whole, the system has advantages and disadvantages. One of the obvious disadvantages is that verses are liable to be quoted out of context, and as a result to lose their real meaning and impact. On the other hand, the divisions sometimes (but not always) help in giving certain fixed points of reference in the history or doctrine of the book concerned.

But how much attention should you give to memorization? How much should you realistically attempt? As with other methods we have examined, this will depend on various personal factors; memory is a highly individual thing. Yet it may be that most Christians aim much too low. In the 1534 edition of his English New Testament, William Tyndale wrote in his prologue to Romans: 'Forasmuch as this epistle is the principal and most excellent part of the New Testament . . . and also a light and a way in unto the whole Scripture, I think it meet that every Christian man know it by rote and without the book'! Bearing in mind that Romans has 433 verses, the whole thing may sound improbable — but is it *impossible*? When a young American called Dawson Trotman was converted at the age of twenty, he determined to memorize Scripture at the rate of one verse a day, with the result that at the end of his first three years as a Christian he knew over 1,000 verses of the Bible off by heart — the equivalent of a passage more than twice the length of Romans. He became so convinced of the value of this that he eventually became the founder of The Navigators, now a world-wide organization promoting systematic Bible study and memorization.

Yet memorizing Scripture is not just for the Dawson Trotmans of this world, nor is it merely a useful device for keeping Sunday School children up to the mark! In Tyndale's words, it is for 'every Christian man'. Not everyone will be able to manage the same amount, of course, but I am convinced that many have an achievement potential much greater than they imagine. There are no inflexible rules about this method of Bible study, but five words sum up some of the most important principles involved.

Firstly, *activation*. Make a start! If you have never tackled memorization seriously before, you might begin by checking how accurately you can quote the Scriptures you think you know. If you find you are not word perfect, work at them until you are. Get someone else to check the results for you, and get ready to notice the first signs of progress!

Secondly, *co-ordination*. Set a target for yourself, and then work out a system for reaching it. Organizations such as The Navigators (their British address is 27 High Street, New Malden, Surrey KT3 4BY) can supply material, but there is no reason why you should not develop one of your own..

Write or type Bible material on cards (classifying them, perhaps, into themes) and try to buy up extra time when these can be read or reviewed. A coffee or lunch break, a train or bus journey, the time spent waiting for an appointment — these and many other odd moments can be used profitably in this way. A cassette recorder can be a tremendous help, too. Not only is it an excellent tool to use at home, but it can also be used in travelling, turning even a brief car journey into another opportunity to learn or review parts of Scripture.

Memorizing individual verses is fine, but if you do this, try to group them into themes, rather than reeling them off in a haphazard way. Subjects immediately applicable to daily living, such as the sovereignty of God, assurance, temptation, prayer, love and the power of the Holy Spirit would be excellent. From individual verses, try to graduate to passages, paragraphs or chapters. Some of the psalms would be easiest at first — say Psalms 1, 23, 51, 95, 121 and 146 — but try to go on to other chapters, such as Isaiah 53, John 3, John 10, Romans 8, Ephesians 2 or Colossians 3. You could do this at the same time as you were engaged in a detailed study of the passage concerned. Finally, you might even set your sights on memorizing a whole book, as some Christians have done, to their tremendous blessing.

Thirdly, *concentration*. There is no escaping the fact that except for the favoured few memorization is not easy. It calls for disciplined, concentrated effort. Yet to recognize this is to go a long way towards overcoming any early discouragement. Keep working at your chosen target; this is an area where practice does make perfect!

Fourthly, *meditation*. As in every other method of Bible study, always remember that you are not handling a cold collection of dead men's writings, but the living Word of the living God. The more you appreciate this, and seek to develop a love for God's Word, the greater the benefit you will receive from your study. What is more, you will discover a direct connection between loving the Bible and learning it. John Whitlock, one of the Puritan preachers ejected from the Church of England in 1662, put it like this in one of the sermons he preached at that time: 'Affection is a very great help to memory ... A man will remember what his mind and heart is set upon. A special means to keep truth in your hearts is to labour that it may be engraven in your hearts. Look upon the Word and ordinances of God as your treasury, and you will then be sure, at least practically, to remember it. Men scarcely forget where they have laid their treasure or their jewels ... Divine meditation fixes truths in the head and fastens them in the heart.'

Fifthly, *application*. No method of Bible study is complete until it is applied, and this is as true of Bible memorization as of any other method. One could presumably teach a parrot to recite Scripture, but of what benefit would that be, even to the parrot? Yet all scriptural income is meant to have a spiritual outcome. The psalmist made this clear when he wrote, 'I have hidden your word in my heart that I might not sin against you' (Psalm 119:11) and it was precisely because he had that purpose firmly fixed in his mind that he was able to add, 'I meditate on your precepts and consider your ways. I delight in your decrees; I will not neglect your word' (Psalm 119:15, 16). Memorizing Scripture makes great demands, but it also yields rich dividends.

For all its length, this chapter has only touched on eight fairly obvious methods of studying the Bible. Of course, not all of them can be followed at once, nor would I suggest keeping permanently to any one method. Think out which one is most likely to meet your own particular need at this time, and tackle that first; then change when you feel that another approach would be helpful.

Some people might feel, after reading this chapter, that

real Bible study calls for time, planning, discipline, concentration and sheer hard work. *It does*, but is that surprising? Paul makes it clear that the way to transformation of the life is by 'the renewing of your mind' (Romans 12:2) and that is not done easily or instantly. Properly approached and applied, Bible study leads to deep and lasting joy, but it is not a Christian entertainment industry; the satisfaction it yields is that which comes to the goldminer, not the sunbather. God does not promise his blessing to the casual Christian who drops in for a chat, but he does promise it to them 'who keep his statutes and seek him with all their heart' (Psalm 119:2). Whatever your methods or means, make sure that you can claim that promise by meeting the conditions.

9.
The outcome of obedience

The straightforward purpose of this book is stated in its title. My one aim has been to encourage the reader of the Bible to *enjoy* it, to bring him to the place where he can say with Jeremiah that the Word of God is 'my joy and my heart's delight' (Jeremiah 15:16). As we saw in the first chapter, unbelievers may find the whole idea of enjoying the Bible either absurd or impossible, but the Christian who knows his Bible knows better. Time and again we are told that one of the great purposes of God speaking to his people is that they might have deep, lasting, spiritual joy. Just a few hours before his crucifixion, Jesus told his dejected disciples that the specific purpose of the teaching he had given them was 'that my joy may be in you and that your joy may be complete' (John 15:11). Later, in praying to his Father, he said that his reason for teaching the disciples in the way he had was 'so that they may have the full measure of my joy within them' (John 17:13). One of the specific reasons John wrote his First Epistle was 'to make your joy complete' (1 John 1:4 footnote). Notice that in all of these instances God's intention is not that his Word might prohibit our joy, but that it might produce it. God has not outlawed rejoicing, nor placed an embargo on enjoyment — as a matter of fact, exactly the opposite is true. The psalmist says, 'Rejoice in the Lord and be glad, you righteous; sing, all you who are upright in heart!' (Psalm 32:11) and 'Sing joyfully to the Lord, you righteous' (Psalm 33:1), while Paul adds, 'Rejoice in the Lord always. I will say it again: Rejoice!' (Philippians 4:4) and 'Be joyful always' (1 Thessalonians 5:16).

These verses tell us something many Christians seem to forget, and that is that to rejoice is actually a duty, something God commands us to do as clearly as he commands us to pray, to worship, to give and to evangelize. To put it as plainly as possible, Christians are under orders to rejoice! As God 'richly provides us with everything for our enjoyment' (1 Timothy 6:17) and as the Bible is one of his greatest gifts, we can be sure that enjoying your Bible has biblical backing.

But what is the link between rejoicing and Bible reading? To rephrase the question, how can reading the Bible lead to the joy a Christian is meant to have? The first way to answer these questions is to be clear about one thing, and that is that reading the Bible does not bring joy *automatically*. Hearing, reading or knowing God's Word is no guarantee of happiness. When Adam heard God speaking to him he cringed behind a tree and cried out, 'I heard . . . and I was afraid' (Genesis 3:10). God repeatedly spoke to the children of Israel in the wilderness but 'the message they heard was of no value to them' (Hebrews 4:2). The rich young ruler who had a personal interview with Jesus 'went away sad' (Mark 10:22). Judas Iscariot heard Christ's preaching for three years and ended up by committing suicide. These four examples alone should be enough to convince us that the Word of God does not automatically bring joy to the person who reads or hears it.

This is obviously true of the unbeliever who reads the Bible and remains unconverted. He may get some kind of satisfaction out of the Bible, by admiring it as a fine piece of literature, or a commendable collection of moral ideals, but he will never discover the joy that is basic to all others, that of being able to say, 'The Lord is my strength and my song; he has become my salvation' (Psalm 118:14).

Yet it is not only unbelievers who can read or study the Scriptures without being blessed. Christians too can come away from the Bible empty, unsatisfied and joyless, and if they were completely honest, many would have to confess that there are times when they do. This merely emphasizes my point: no amount of reading, study or analysis of the pages of Scripture will automatically result in the joy we ought to know. Nobody, for instance, will find their life enriched merely by knowing what we might call the *physical* facts contained in the Bible. There is no great joy in discovering the dimensions of Noah's ark, the diet of John the Baptist or the distance from Jerusalem to Bethany. But we can go further. There is no automatic enrichment of life to be gained from accumulating the Bible's *spiritual* facts. It is possible for a person to acquire an encyclopaedic knowledge of what the Bible has to say about God, man, sin, salvation, heaven and a dozen other doctrines, and be not one whit better or happier as a result. Finally, no man is automatically better for knowing the *moral* facts contained in the Bible — its standards, ethics, directives, warnings and commandments. To personalize this for a moment, you could recite the Beatitudes (Matthew 5:3–12) to perfection and not experience a single one of the joyful blessings which are promised in them. You could master the text of the Bible in its original languages yet know little or nothing of its touch and power in your everyday life. 'He who has ears, let him hear' (Matthew 11:15).

Then what is the connection between Bible study and the joy that it is meant to bring? What is the vital link that brings them together? The answer to these questions is the theme of this final chapter, and it can be summed up in one word — *obedience*. Joy is the natural outcome of the

Christian's obedience to the revealed will of God. Before
we develop this principle, let us be sure that it is firmly
rooted in the Bible itself. That presents no problem. One
of the psalmists tells us, 'Blessed are they who maintain
justice, who constantly do what is right' (Psalm 106:3),
while the psalm which speaks of God's Word more than
any other part of the Bible begins, 'Blessed are they whose
ways are blameless, who walk according to the law of the
Lord. Blessed are they who keep his statutes and seek
him with all their heart' (Psalm 119:1, 2). While giving
his disciples some of his most profound teaching, Jesus
specifically added the words: 'Now that you know these
things, you will be blessed if you do them' (John 13:17).
On another occasion he told a woman who commented
on the joy that Mary must have had in being his mother:
'Blessed rather are those who hear the word of God and
obey it' (Luke 11:28). The ever-practical James, after
stating that the man who does no more than read the
Bible is deceiving himself, goes on to say, 'But the man
who looks intently into the perfect law that gives free-
dom, and continues to do this, not forgetting what he
has heard, but doing it — he will be blessed in what he
does' (James 1:25). On the very first page of the Bible
we are told of Adam and Eve, living as they then were
in perfect obedience to God's will, that 'God blessed
them' (Genesis 1:28); and on the very last page we are
told, 'Blessed is he who keeps the words of the prophecy
in this book' (Revelation 22:7). From Genesis to Revelation, then, we find this principle firmly established: joy
is not to be seen or sought in isolation, something that
can be acquired on our own terms, or without any reference to what the Bible says or to the way we live. It is
the natural, promised result of obedience to the Word
of God.

Yet the word 'obedience' sounds legalistic, stark,
mechanical and somehow unrelated to the whole idea of

joy. It is only when we examine it more closely in the light of Scripture that it begins to come alive. Let us look at five aspects of the biblical picture of obedience.

Firstly, it is willing obedience. If there is a single statement in the Bible that could be said to be pivotal on the whole subject of obedience, then it is surely the one Jesus made when answering the Jews who were questioning the source of his teaching. This is what he said: 'If anyone chooses to do God's will, he will find out whether my teaching comes from God or whether I speak on my own' (John 7:17). The word 'chooses' has in it an element of strong determination or resolution. It speaks not of a soft option, but of the determined desire of the heart. Nothing is more important at this point than to get a firm and clear grasp of what this means. Think it through carefully and you will realize it is exactly the opposite of what we might expect. The Bible does not teach that an increasing understanding of its origin or meaning will result in our having a greater willingness to obey it, but rather that a greater willingness to obey it will result in a clearer grasp of its authority and integrity, leading to a greater understanding of its meaning. The correct biblical sequence of the three key words here is not understanding, willingness and obedience, but willingness, understanding and obedience. Knowing what God's Word is saying to us at any point in our lives does not necessarily mean that we become willing to obey it, but if we come to the Bible sincerely willing to do whatever God commands, he will graciously give us a deepening understanding of its meaning. As J. C. Ryle put it, 'God tests men's sincerity by making obedience part of the process by which religious knowledge is obtained. Are we really willing to do God's will so far as we know it? If we are, God will take care that our knowledge is increased.'[1]

It is obviously true that we can only obey what we know; and in God's economy a true spiritual understanding of what God is saying to us will be granted if we first have a determined willingness to obey what he is saying. In the words of Donald Grey Barnhouse, 'The shortest road to an understanding of the Bible is the acceptance of the fact that God is speaking in every line. The shortest road to the knowledge of the will of God is the willingness to do that will even before we know it.'[2]

Secondly, it is loving obedience. This is closely locked into the point about willingness, and in one sense forms the very basis of it. In the clearest possible words Jesus said, 'If you love me, you will obey what I command' (John 14:15) and, of course, this principle covers not only the specific words he spoke while here on earth, but the whole body of biblical teaching. To tie both principles in together, we could say this: just as willingness to obey is a test of our integrity, so obedience itself is a test of our love. No New Testament writer puts this across more firmly than the apostle John, and he makes his point both negatively and positively. Negatively, he says this: 'If anyone loves the world, the love of the Father is not in him' (1 John 2:15). 'Anyone who does not love his brother, whom he has seen, cannot love God, whom he has not seen' (1 John 4:20). Positively, he puts it like this: 'Those who obey [God's] commands live in him, and he in them' (1 John 3:24); 'If we love each other, God lives in us and his love is made complete in us' (1 John 4:12). Finally, he clinches the point with this simple, definitive statement: 'This is love for God: to obey his commands' (1 John 5:3).

Whole volumes could be written here about the relationship between law and love, but in the context of this book only one thing needs to be underlined, and that is that the Christian's love for God and his obedience to God's revealed will are inextricably locked together. Obedience is the measure of his love, and love is the motive for his obedience. In other words, biblical obedience is based on love, not legalism. The Christian should seek to obey God's

Word, not because he is terrified of God, but because he is
devoted to him. This is an important test of a person's
true spirituality, and one you should be careful to apply
to your own heart and life. Is your obedience based on
the fear of regulations, or is it the fruit of a relationship?
There is certainly no joy in obedience when it is merely a
slavish attempt to follow a book of rules, but only when
it is the natural outcome of love, devotion, worship. And
what is the basis of these? Nothing less than God's amazing
love for us. Obedience has been described as 'the response
of love to the gracious initiative of God'. This is exactly
what Paul meant when he urged Christians to present
themselves 'as living sacrifices, holy and pleasing to God',
because the whole basis of his impassioned plea was 'in
view of God's mercy' (Romans 12:1). Christians are to
obey as an expression of their love for God, and 'We love
because he first loved us' (1 John 4:19). Biblical obedience
springs from gratitude for grace; it is *loving obedience*.

Thirdly, it is believing obedience. As we saw earlier,
the children of Israel were among those who failed to
benefit as they should from hearing the Word of God,
and at this point it is important to notice exactly why
that was so. We are specifically told that 'The message
they heard was of no value to them, *because those who
heard did not combine it with faith*' (Hebrews 4:2). The
reference, of course, is to the Israelites' repeated failure
to trust the promises of God, with the tragic result that,
other than Joshua and Caleb (who did believe God), none
of that particular generation actually entered the promised
land of Canaan. Commenting on this verse, the nineteenth-
century Scottish preacher, Dr John Brown wrote, 'It is by
believing a principle that it becomes influential, and it is
by digesting food that it becomes nutritive. Food not
mingled with the mass of vital fluids, in consequence of
the process of digestion, does not serve its purpose. Truth,
unless believed, mingled with the springs of moral action,

cannot serve its purpose either.'[3] The language may be a little dated, but the point is well made. The primary reference is to hearing the gospel, where the application is obvious. A person may hear the good news of salvation a thousand times, but unless there is the response of living faith, the person concerned will never be saved. As the same writer says a little later, 'Without faith it is impossible to please God, because anyone who comes to him must believe that he exists and that he rewards those who earnestly seek him' (Hebrews 11:6).

Yet the same principle has a much wider application. God places a tremendous premium on faith at every point in a Christian's life, so much so that Jesus' words to the two blind men can be taken as a permanent principle: 'According to your faith will it be done to you' (Matthew 9:29). The Bible teems with promises of blessing that God makes to his people, but unless you believe them and act upon them in faith, you will never know those blessings in your own experience. You may go through an empty outward form of observance, but unless it is mingled with those 'vital fluids' of faith, the blessing will not follow. Dr Billy Graham gives a vivid example of this in his autobiography. He tells how in August 1949 he became filled with doubts about the Bible. He preached it as clearly as he knew how, but every time he quoted from it he found himself wondering whether its statements were true. The result was disastrous: in his own words, 'My ministry had gone.' That summer, he took his Bible up into the Sierra Nevada mountains of California, and thought long and hard over the whole issue. Finally, he gave in to God. Getting on his knees he cried out, 'Father, I cannot understand many things in this book, I cannot come intellectually all the way, but I accept it by faith to be the authoritative, inspired Word of the living God.' Immediately, those 'vital fluids' began to work, and as Dr Graham himself puts it, 'A month later, in Los Angeles, I found that this book had become a sword in my hand.'

Biblical obedience is believing obedience. It is not cold, clinical conformity to a code of ethics; it is willing moral action based on a spiritual attitude, and that attitude is one of absolute trust in the authority and integrity of God, and therefore of every word he has spoken. What is more, this is the attitude with which we should begin, not merely one at which we should aim. In his book *'Fundamentalism' and the Word of God*, Dr J. I. Packer puts it like this: 'Is it reasonable to take God's Word and believe that he has spoken the truth, even though I cannot fully comprehend what he has said? The question carries its own answer. We should not abandon faith in anything that God has taught us merely because we cannot solve all the problems which it raises. Our own intellectual competence is not the test and measure of divine truth. It is not for us to stop believing because we lack understanding, or to postpone believing till we can get understanding, but to believe in order that we may understand.' In a biblical response to the Bible, faith, willingness, understanding and obedience are all bound up together.

Fourthly, it is whole-hearted obedience. For the sake of brevity, we can use this single statement to cover both the *scope* and the *spirit* of biblical obedience. As to the *scope*, the point is not even open for discussion. From beginning to end the Bible makes it clear that man is under an inescapable obligation to obey God in everything. Under the Old Covenant, the requirement was clear and uncompromising. Reminding the Israelites of the Ten Commandments, Moses told them, 'So be careful to do what the Lord your God has commanded you; do not turn aside to the right or to the left. Walk in *all* the way that the Lord your God has commanded you . . .' (Deuteronomy 5:32, 33). When Joshua took over the leadership of the nation the requirement remained the same: 'Do not let this Book of the Law depart from your mouth; meditate on it day and night, so that you may be careful to do everything written in it. Then you will be prosperous and successful' (Joshua 1:8). In the New Testament, we find Paul concerned that the Christians at Corinth should be 'obedient in *everything*' (2 Corinthians 2:9) and later in the same letter he says, 'We take captive *every* thought to make it obedient to Christ' (2 Corinthians 10:5). The Christian is not entitled to pick and choose his virtues, but is under a moral and spiritual obligation to exercise and develop every one of them. Having reminded his readers of the 'very great and precious promises' that God had given them in their calling and election as Christians, Peter went on to urge them, 'For this very reason, make every effort to add to your faith goodness; and to goodness, knowledge; and to knowledge, self-control; and to self-control, perseverance; and to perseverance, godliness; and to godliness, brotherly kindness; and to brotherly kindness, love' (2 Peter 1:5–8). Notice that these are not offered as alternatives, nor do they form a general list from which every Christian is allowed to make his own personal choice. The linking word is 'and', not 'or'; obedience is meant to be total, not partial. The Christian who is genuinely seeking the joy that comes from knowing the blessing of God on his life will be concerned to obey *all* of his commands, heed *all* of his warnings and trust *all* of his promises.

But whole-hearted obedience embraces not only its scope but its *spirit*, and again we can quickly find a biblical basis to make the point. In the same context from which we quoted earlier, Moses told the Israelites, 'The Lord your God commands you this day to follow these decrees and laws; carefully observe them *with all your heart* and with all your soul' (Deuteronomy 26:16). When Jesus was asked which was the most important of all the commandments, he replied, 'The most important one is this: "Hear, O Israel, the Lord our God, the Lord is one. Love the Lord your God *with all your heart* and with all your

soul and with all your mind and with all your strength"'
(Mark 12:29, 30). Rejoicing at the miraculous change that
had taken place in their lives following their conversion,
Paul wrote to the Romans, 'Thanks be to God that, though
you used to be slaves to sin, you *whole-heartedly* obeyed
the form of teaching to which you were entrusted'
(Romans 6:17).

Notice that these statements again help to deliver us
from thinking of obedience to the Bible's teaching as
being a mechanical formula. It is more than that: it is
something that springs from the heart because it is the
result of a relationship. The Christian seeks to obey the
Bible not because he knows the book, but because he
knows the Author; and when he remembers that the
Author is the eternal God of glory, who has given him
new life through the death of his Son, enabled him to
repent and believe, granted him the forgiveness of sins
and eternal life, adopted him into his eternal family,
sent the Holy Spirit into his heart to guide and strengthen
him, rescued him from hell and promised him a place in
heaven, surely we should expect his obedience to be
grateful, glad and *whole-hearted*? Every Christian who
comes to the Bible with these truths in mind will want
to say with Philip Doddridge,

> My gracious Lord I own thy right
> To every service I can pay;
> And call it my supreme delight
> To hear thy dictates and obey.

Fifthly, it is dependent obedience. It might seem that
the four aspects of obedience already mentioned are
sufficient to give us a working grasp of what is involved
in obeying the Bible's teaching. Yet there is one final
aspect that is so important that it governs all the others,
and that is that biblical obedience is *dependent*. The

simplest way to approach this is by honest testimony, by looking at the ideal and the actual. To bring the whole issue on to a personal basis, how does your own experience match up to the pattern the Bible lays down? Just check through the four points we have studied together. Obedience should be *willing*; but is yours always so? Do you always leap at doing God's will, or are there times when you seem to have moral lead in your boots and drag heavily along, trying to do the right thing but finding it nothing more than a weary duty? Obedience should be *loving*; is yours? Do you live at a constant pitch of spiritual enthusiasm, with your heart on fire with love for Christ? Or are there times when the flame burns low? Obedience should be *believing*; but can that always be said of yours? Do you really trust God completely in every issue of life? Do you constantly and literally take him at his word? Or are you sometimes ashamed at your lack of faith? Obedience should be *whole-hearted*; can you claim perfection in that area? Can you honestly say that with all your heart you are always obedient to God's Word? Or is it not the simple truth that, although you know it should be otherwise, your obedience is at times erratic and half-hearted?

As this is a book, and not a live discussion, I will not, of course, be able to hear your answers; but if you are being honest, I do know what they are, and that they will be the same as mine! I know that, along with every other Christian in the world, we find that we are spiritual battlefields, with our minds, wills, spirits, consciences, hearts and bodies caught up in a fierce and apparently never-ending conflict between good and evil. The battle see-saws to and fro in a swirling mass of thoughts, emotions, desires, hopes, fears and actions. Sometimes it swings violently from one extreme to another; at one moment we feel we have the devil himself on the run, yet in no time at all we are broken and defeated. Let me give you a vivid biblical illustration of this very kind of thing. At one point in the life of the great prophet Elijah, he took on 850 heathen prophets single-handed, and was so confident of victory that he could afford to mock them, almost play with them. Yet soon after his astonishing triumph, one word from Jezebel was enough to send him skulking into the desert in a state of abject depression (see 1 Kings 18:17–19:4).

It is Paul who gives us the fullest theological explanation of all of this, and he majors on it in two particular passages. The shortest and clearest of these is this: 'The sinful nature desires what is contrary to the Spirit, and the Spirit what is contrary to the sinful nature. They are in conflict with each other, so that you do not do what you want' (Galatians 5:17). Here the two opponents are identified. One is our sinful nature, which we inherited as part of our humanity, and the other is the Holy Spirit, who came to dwell within us at the time of our conversion. One dates from the time of our natural birth and the other from the time of our new birth, and both are now locked together in deadly combat.

In the other passage, Paul states the same truth by way of testimony. The complete section of Scripture involved is rather complex but three phrases are particularly significant here. In the first, Paul recognizes and condemns his old sinful nature: 'I know that nothing good lives in me, that is, in my sinful nature' (Romans 7:18). In the second, he rejoices that the Holy Spirit has brought new, godly desires into his life: 'In my inner being I delight in God's law' (Romans 7:22). In the third, he spells out the inevitable outcome of these two opposing forces at work within him: 'So then, I myself in my mind am a slave to God's law, but in the sinful nature a slave to the law of sin' (Romans 7:25).

Is that not also your honest testimony? You accept without question that the Bible is the Word of God, you rejoice in its glory, majesty and purity and you long with all your heart to obey it in every detail, to find your life running parallel to its teachings at every point. Yet is it not true that, left to your own efforts, you cannot turn that passion into practice, and that, like Paul, you find yourself all too often doing the things you ought not to do, and not doing the things you ought to do? Then you should have no difficulty in accepting this final crucial point, that in rendering the obedience to the Bible that will bring joy into your life you are utterly dependent upon God's enabling. He alone is the dynamic of all his demands. In Paul's words, 'It is God who works in you to will and to act according to his good purpose' (Philippians 2:13).

But does this mean that you have no responsibility in the matter? Do you just 'let go and let God'? Not at all! The Bible makes it clear that the Christian is to fight, to wrestle, to watch, to be diligent. He does not get taken to heaven in a hammock! Yet at the end of the day, all his fighting, wrestling, watching and diligence will be in vain unless they are done in a power other than his own. The psalmist captures this tension of truths in a single sentence: 'Direct me in the path of your commands, for there I find delight' (Psalm 119:35). Notice how the various elements we have mentioned are included in that one statement. He sees the path before him, knows it is right, longs to walk in it, and, in an immediate recognition of his own chronic weakness, cries out to God to be given the power to do so. He realizes that his obedience is constantly dependent on God's gracious enabling to subdue his sinful nature and ungodly desires and to lead him day by day in the ways of righteousness, peace and joy. Over 2,000 years later, Robert Robinson put it like this:

> Oh, to grace how great a debtor
> Daily I'm constrained to be!
> Let that grace, Lord, like a fetter,
> Bind my wandering heart to thee:
> Prone to wander, Lord, I feel it,
> Prone to leave the God I love;
> Take my heart, Oh, take and seal it,
> Seal it from thy courts above!

When you come to the Scriptures in that kind of spirit, and God hears and answers that kind of prayer, one thing is certain: you *will* enjoy your Bible!

Notes

Introduction
1. J. I. Packer, *God has Spoken*

Chapter 2
1. A. W. Pink, *Gleanings from Genesis*
2. F. J. A. Hort and B. F. Westcott, *The New Testament in the Original Greek*
3. F. G. B. Kenyon, *Our Bible and the Ancient Manuscripts*
4. A. H. Sayce, *Monument Facts and Higher Critical Fancies*
5. *ibid.*
6. G. C. Aalders, *A Short Introduction to the Pentateuch*

Chapter 3
1. W. Hendriksen, *A Commentary on 1 and 2 Timothy and Titus*
2. J. I. Packer, *God has Spoken*
3. J. C. Ryle, *Expository Thoughts on the Gospels*

Chapter 4
1. F. W. Albright, *The Christian Century,* 19 November 1958
2. N. Glueck, *Rivers in the Desert; History of Neteg*
3. P. W. Stoner, *Science Speaks*
4. J. Calvin, *Institutes of the Christian Religion*

Chapter 5
1. Quoted by Sir Robert Anderson, *The Bible and Modern Criticism*

Chapter 7
1. Elisabeth Elliot, *Shadow of the Almighty*
2. A. W. Tozer, *The Pursuit of God*

Chapter 8
1. G. H. Lang, *An Ordered Life*
2. G. H. Lang, *ibid.*

Chapter 9
1. J. C. Ryle, *Expository Thoughts on the Gospels*
2. D. G. Barnhouse, *Words Fitly Spoken*
3. J. Brown, *An Exposition of the Epistle to the Hebrews*